BARDA BALKA

Monolith from west (pl. 3)

BARDA BALKA

by

BRUCE HOWE†

with Foreword by

Yorke M. Rowan

ORIENTAL INSTITUTE COMMUNICATIONS • NUMBER 31
THE ORIENTAL INSTITUTE OF THE UNIVERSITY OF CHICAGO
CHICAGO • ILLINOIS

Library of Congress Control Number: 2013943111
ISBN-10: 1-61491-000-6
ISBN-13: 978-1-61491-000-8
ISSN: 0146-678X

The Oriental Institute, Chicago

Published 2014. Printed in the United States of America.

Oriental Institute Communications 31

Series Editors

Leslie Schramer *and* Thomas G. Urban

assisted by

Rebecca Cain *and* Zuhal Kuru Sharp

Director Gil J. Stein, Gretel Braidwood, and Raymond Tindel assisted in the production of this volume.

Cover Illustration
The monolith from the west. See pl. 3

Printed by Thomson-Shore, Dexter, Michigan

The paper used in this publication meets the minimum requirements of American National Standard for Information Services — Permanence of Paper for Printed Library Materials, ANSI Z39.48-1984.

∞

TABLE OF CONTENTS

ABBREVIATIONS

B.P.	before present	etc.	*et cetera*, and so forth
cm	centimeter(s)	fig(s).	figure(s)
e.g.	*exempli gratia*, for example	m	meter(s)
et al.	*et alii*, and others	pl(s).	plate(s)

FIGURES

TABLES

PLATES

FOREWORD

Yorke M. Rowan, The Oriental Institute

The origins and diversification of the genus *Homo* during the Lower Paleolithic (> 2.5–0.3 million years ago) witnessed the expansion of early hominids beyond Africa and into Eurasia during a period of transition from a warm, stable Pliocene climate to the colder, variable Pleistocene climate (Shea 2013, p. 47). During this long period, techniques and artifact forms remained largely similar wherever hominids lived. In contrast, Middle Paleolithic assemblages demonstrated much greater distinctiveness between regions, with changes in the lithic technology that appear to follow different regional trajectories. During the Middle Paleolithic, behavioral complexity emerges that includes big-game hunting, bodily adornment, symbolic behavior (e.g., mortuary goods), heat-treatment of lithic materials, and use of bone tools. The underlying evolutionary processes involved in these profound behavioral changes are widely debated.

The discovery of Neanderthal burials at Shanidar Cave, in the Zagros Mountains of northern Iraq (Solecki 1971), and the possible evidence for ritual behavior associated with these burials, meant that the Zagros Mousterian is now found in most textbooks or discussions of the Paleolithic. Despite the extensive debate about deposition of flowers and other evidence for ritual at Shanidar, research into the Mousterian of the Zagros soon lagged far behind that of the Levant. Lindly (2005) attributes this to two factors. First, new dating techniques applied to stone and bone dated the appearance of anatomically modern humans in the Levant to more than 100,000 years ago. Second, political instability in Iraq has largely curtailed excavations and surveys. With evidence in the Levant for the possible overlap of archaic hominids and anatomically modern *Homo sapiens*, and little in the way of new discoveries in the Zagros, attention concentrated elsewhere. Yet as an intersection between the Levant, Europe, and Asia, the Zagros is an important region to understand the Middle Paleolithic of southwest Asia, particularly the generally high-altitude adaptations during colder environmental conditions that provide an essential counterpoint to those of other regions.

Despite the limited time in the field at Barda Balka, the site was relatively rich (see pls. 5–22) and apparently well excavated by the standards of the times. The thorough description by Bruce Howe and the fine artifact illustrations establish this as one of the rare studies of a Lower/Middle Paleolithic site in the region. Nonetheless, new dating techniques, scientific advances, and a reevaluation of older techniques require a few cautionary points in order to contextualize the Barda Balka assemblage within more recent interpretations. This is aided in large measure by the dissertation research and subsequent publication on the Zagros Mousterian by John M. Lindly (2005). Lindly studied material and collated the data from seven Mousterian sites in the Zagros, comparing them to each other and to Mousterian sites in other regions, specifically, the Levant and the Transcaucasus. As part of that study, Lindly conducted a highly detailed analysis of the Barda Balka assemblage, specifically focusing on the flakes and cores in order to understand the procurement, reduction, and curation of the assemblage, and to compare it to other Mousterian sites. Analysis in detail is unnecessary here, but his study is very important to situate Barda Balka and to update the site in light of more recent evidence and current debates.

Dating the Middle Paleolithic has been problematic until recently, primarily because the sites are typically beyond the range of radiocarbon dating, which is limited to approximately 50,000 years ago. Although other techniques, such as thermoluminescence (TL), electron spin resonance (ESR), and uranium-series decay, have resolved many chronological issues, sites excavated before the development of these techniques remain difficult to locate in chronologies.

Based on geomorphological deposits, Howe dates Barda Balka to between the last interglacial stage and the early glacial periods of the Middle Paleolithic, possibly between 60 and 100/120 thousand years ago. Although we are without absolute dates for the site, this estimation is no longer very likely. The dates of the Middle Paleolithic should be pushed back to between 245 and 45/47 thousand years ago, which better conforms to the Late Acheulean industry Howe recognized at the site.

More importantly, the assignment to the last interglacial or early part of the last glacial is difficult to substantiate. It is just as likely (and possibly more likely) that the gravels date to a late interstadial/stadial of the penultimate glaciation (oxygen isotope stages 7/8), pushing this back to ca. 250,000 B.P. or earlier. The presence of the bifacial Acheulean handaxes support these earlier dates. One of the defining characteristics of Acheulean assemblages is the significant numbers of large cutting tools (Shea 2013, p. 73). By the Middle Paleolithic, smaller and thinner blanks are produced for subsequent retouch into a wider range of tool types.

Lindly mentions that Barda Balka marks the first occurrence of handaxes in the Zagros since those discovered by Dorothy Garrod at Hazar Merd (Garrod 1930). As part of his dissertation, Lindly studied the flake component of Barda Balka, and his observations, summarized here, rely on his intensive analysis of the assemblage.

Lindly's study suggests that the Mousterian sites of the Zagros are typologically very similar, with the exception of Barda Balka, which has a higher frequency of denticulates and notches than scrapers. He further acknowledges that other Zagros sites do not contain choppers or handaxes, which would suggest earlier dates for Barda Balka than other Mousterian sites. The large amount of tool resharpening that Lindly recognized at the Zagros Mousterian sites makes them typologically distinct from the better-known Levantine assemblages. He suggests that the pointed artifacts of the Zagros Mousterian differ from those of the Levantine Mousterian primarily because of the more intensive resharpening. Whereas the Levantine Levallois points are created as pointed blanks and lack intensive resharpening, the Zagros points (whether convergent scrapers or Mousterian points) are retouched or resharpened to achieve the final pointed tool. Lindly remains ambivalent about whether these were pointed flakes to begin with, and he is clearly unconvinced that convergent-edged artifacts — manufactured or retouched — were being used as projectile points. There is a problem in this approach, however, because Lindly (2005, pp. 40–41) rejects the utility of identifying the use of the Levallois techniques (or their absence). This becomes particularly critical when discussing points because Levallois points tend to be more standardized and a more efficient use of resources.

Further comparison between the Zagros and Levantine Mousterian industries produce other distinctions. Lindly (2005, p. 90) finds that flakes are smaller in the Zagros than in the Levant, yet they are similar in shape, and the length/width ratios and width/thickness ratios of some industries are very similar. The length of flake platforms and widths are smaller for Zagros samples as well, with a higher proportion of plain platforms in the Zagros industries. The higher number of non-cortical flakes in the Zagros industries may also reflect smaller size of parent material and greater reduction (ibid., p. 91). Lindly also notes that the cores from the Zagros Mousterian industries are smaller than those from the Levantine, in virtually every dimension (ibid. p. 26). Zagros cores also have lower percentage of cortical cores. Regional sources will determine size constraints (smaller pebbles produce smaller flakes). Since different raw material sources in each region can determine the size of subsequent by products, and other qualities are similar, similar reduction strategies are apparently employed in both regions.

Despite these similarities in reduction techniques, the Mousterian industries of the Zagros and Levant are quite distinct typologically. With a much larger sample and more intensive investigations, the Levant includes a variety of type sites, including hunting camps, quarries, and base-camp locales. The Zagros sites analyzed by Lindly suggest sites that were primarily short occupation hunting/base camps occupied, briefly, by small groups. Yet the differences, he argues, are primarily related to differences in raw material and intensity of reduction rather than significant distinctions between core reduction strategies. If that is accurate, the great diversity of adaptations to different environments and elevations is not necessarily reflected in the core reduction technologies of archaic hominids in southwest Asia. Here again, however, Levallois techniques are key to understanding core reduction technologies and Lindly's rejection of Levallois techniques would affect the ability to connect core reduction to adaptations.

Comparison to the northwest Caucasus (Azerbaijan, Armenia, Georgia, southern Russia), a similar montane ecosystem, would make a more appropriate comparison with the Zagros, but the reporting of Transcaucasian sites is inconsistent, lacking technological details concerning flake, tool, and core sizes. Bifaces found at Mezmaiskaya (Russia, near the Black Sea) further indicate that this is a standard tool type in Middle Paleolithic assemblages in central and southwest Asia. Lindly also points out that tools produced at low elevations do not seem to differ significantly from those at higher elevations. Again, raw material apparently limited technology such that similar lithic assemblages are found in both Caucasus and Zagros Mousterian sites. Lindly concludes by noting that although the Middle Paleolithic industries in the Zagros are distinct from those in the Levant, this is largely a consequence of a generally smaller size and more intensive reduction and resharpening (2005, p. 94) and does not necessarily reflect different populations or cultures. By the same token, Lindly argues that similarities between sites in the Zagros and those in the Caucasus and central Asia reflect comparable raw materials and the same high elevations where sites in the two regions are located. Interaction between the regions and the Middle Paleolithic populations is also possible.

Seasonality is a key issue for the Zagros Middle Paleolithic sites. The Pleistocene environment would have been substantially different from current conditions, and some sites in the Zagros would have been uninhabitable during the colder periods of the Upper Pleistocene. Barda Balka and Shanidar are located approximately at the Pleistocene treeline, according to Lindly (2005, pp. 18–19). Seasonality studies were conducted for the Levantine Mousterian, and similar studies could help determine whether or not the Zagros Middle Paleolithic sites were summer occupations.

Lindly argues that sites such as Shanidar, Bisitun, and Barda Balka were probably summer locations rather than base camps, representing only one part of a larger settlement-subsistence system. Located at higher elevations (from 740 to over 2,000 m), he points out that these sites were unlikely to be occupied during a winter in the Pleistocene, and that even summer seasons may have been brief and limited to mild climatic interglacials. Even today these areas are difficult to reach and caves are blocked by snow, and the snow line would have been at lower elevations during much of the Pleistocene.

Relying on analogous movement of historical and modern mobile human groups, Lindly argues that the mobility system would have been similar even in the distant past. As a consequence, occupations of upland sites would have occurred during the summer months, and the lowlands during the fall, winter, and spring. Group sizes during the summer would have been smaller, with high residential mobility. Family groups of foraging archaic hominids possibly scavenged ungulate carcasses, or perhaps hunted migratory herds (that they possibly followed from the lowlands).

As Lindly points out, if the Zagros Mousterian sites were summer camps, then much remains to be learned about what was going on during the rest of the year, presumably in the lowlands. Lowland Mousterian sites are known but have not yet been systematically studied; Levallois cores apparently dominate these lowland sites (Hole and Flannery 1967, p. 156; Lindly 2005, p. 96), suggesting those sites may prove to be quite different in contrast to the upland sites. The use of Levallois technology to discriminate these areas, one which he eschews as a discriminating factor in other aspects of his study, is incorporated.

Tools were apparently resharpened, and cores were small and heavily reduced. Lindly concludes that his analysis supports the resharpening model of Dibble (1987, 1995), arguing that single, double, convergent, and déjeté scrapers fit a resharpening trajectory. Large numbers of heavily resharpened tools, dominated by scrapers and points, is characteristic of the Zagros Mousterian. A notable lack of large, unretouched flakes suggests that people used these as quickly as they were manufactured. Moreover, Lindly suggests that larger flakes and tools sometimes served as cores for the creation of small flakes, indicative of possible scarcity of raw materials. This is supported by some evidence for the movement of cores, given their very low proportion to flakes and tools at some sites. At the same time, other sites have much higher proportions of cores relative to flakes and tools, suggesting that flakes or tools were carried to different locations where they were discarded. If this scenario is accurate, it suggests planning and recognition of future needs for raw material.

Sites with high numbers of retouched tools relative to cores suggest the importance of maintaining or curating tools over manufacture, and possible limitations on access to raw material. Sites with specialized activities reflect this type of pattern. In contrast, sites such as Barda Balka, with higher numbers of cores relative to flakes and tools, emphasize blank and tool manufacture, possibly reflecting more general occupations, possibly residential or multi-purpose.

In contrast to the Levantine Mousterian sites, where hundreds of thousands of lithics are recovered, Lindly views the lithic density at Zagros sites as relatively low, suggesting either short occupational periods, or limited production of new tools, or both. There are other possible factors involved as well, however, such as early excavations where artifacts were thrown away, off-site core processing, conservation of raw material, or site function. These factors, as well as group size in upland sites, could affect the density of lithics.

The density of faunal remains is also quite low. This too could be explained by poor sampling or brief occupations. Nonetheless, the highly fragmentary nature of the fauna suggests intensive processing to extract the maximum sustenance. Combined with the lithic data above, these strategies reflect an attempt to maximize the resources in an area in a relatively expedient manner by foraging archaic hominids, primarily during the summer months.

A final cautionary note is warranted. Although Howe mentions the identification of blood residue almost in passing, we must treat this claim with great caution. Thomas Loy, one of the leaders and main proponents of blood residue analysis, initially crystallized hemoglobin in order to identify blood traces (1983) and later shifted to immunological tests for direct detection of blood proteins (Newman and Julig 1989; Newman et al. 1993). Later in the 1990s, confusing results were reported (Downs and Lowenstein 1995; Eisele et al. 1995), throwing doubt on earlier optimistic interpretations. Some tests determined that blood buried in dry soils preserves for up to only ten months, while blood in damp dirt leaves no blood-residue traces after only one month. In fact, even blood stored eight years in a clean, closed bottle in a laboratory had dropped to only 30–40 percent of immunological and enzymatic activity of the blood proteins, dropping to around 10 percent within months after the bottle was opened (Sensabaugh, Wilson, and Kirk 1971). Even under very arid conditions, blood showed degradation in less than a year (Eisele et al. 1995).

As we would expect from a site excavated in the 1950s, major questions remain. Perhaps the single largest question regards the dates of Barda Balka. Despite the careful comparison to other Middle Paleolithic sites by Lindly, the assemblage from Barda Balka stands because of the Acheulean bifaces. This technological element suggests a Lower Paleolithic, Late Acheulean date, a hypothesis that could be tested with a future investigation. With this publication of Barda Balka an important site is finally available to scholars and will hopefully stimulate new investigations into this poorly understood period of human evolution.

ACKNOWLEDGMENTS

Barda Balka was excavated by Bruce Howe and Herbert E. Wright Jr. during a four-day period in 1951. Howe submitted the final manuscript on the Barda Balka excavations and his findings in the mid-1990s; however, the manuscript was too short to be considered for stand-alone publication. Bruce Howe was born November 20, 2012, and died February 29, 2012. Howe did not leave acknowledgments for this manuscript. Herbert E. Wright Jr., in his 90s at press time, is professor emeritus at the University of Minnesota.

In 2012, with an interest in excavating anew in Kurdistan, the series editors brought Howe's manuscript to Oriental Institute Director Gil J. Stein's attention. Gil asked the editors to inquire about Barda Balka with museum registration, archives, and photography and to ask Research Associate Yorke Rowan's opinion on the manuscript. The result of these inquiries was the addition of more than twenty pages, and the volume is now ready to stand alone.

Yorke M. Rowan very kindly added Barda Balka to his long list of active projects. His *Foreword* was written to address the evolution in scholarship regarding the dating of Barda Balka since the time the manuscript was written. Yorke wishes to express his gratitude to Gary Rollefson for his help.

Oriental Institute Registrars Helen McDonald and Susan Allison, working with Yorke, identified the objects featured on the plates of the manuscript among the thousands of Barda Balka objects housed here. Helen and Susan then registered them (see *Concordance*). During the review of the material in registration, Leslie Schramer took reference photos of most of the many objects from Barda Balka in the collections of the Oriental Institute (pls. 17–22).

Photographer Anna R. Ressman produced new color photography of the objects drawn by Howe (pls. 7a–15a) as well as additional shots of representative artifact types (pl. 16).

John A. Larson, museum archivist, added two pages of previously unpublished photography (pls. 1–2) taken by Gustavus Swift Jr., presumably during excavations in May 1951.

As with any manuscript, we had questions that only the excavators and author could answer. Herbert Wright's memory of the site and its excavation proved quite valuable. There were also several e-mail exchanges with the institution with which Howe had been associated in the search for original documentation. Joseph Greene and Patricia Kervick searched the archives at the Peabody Museum (Harvard University), but no records were found. On the advice of Gretel Braidwood, we wrote to Bruce's nephew, John Howe, and his niece Kate Rantilla very kindly made a gift of his notes and drafts, which were sent to us in Howe's own briefcase, where they had been kept; these are now archived at the Oriental Institute — one document proved useful: a draft of the plan of the excavations (fig. 2). The draft of figure 2 revealed how Trench 1 was determined to be about 50 meters in length.

We thank all those who gave so generously of their time and efforts to help bring this well-deserving publication to light, especially Gretel Braidwood and Ray Tindel, who put us in touch with Bruce Howe's relatives and helped with the identifications of the 1951 excavation team members (pls. 1–2).

Series Editors
Oriental Institute Publications
June 2014

BIBLIOGRAPHY

al-Asil, Naji

1949 "Barda Balka." *Sumer* 5: 205–06.

Bar-Yosef, Ofer, and N. Goren-Inbar

1993 "The Lithic Assemblage of Ubeidiya: A Lower Palaeolithic Site in the Jordan Valley." *Qedem* 34, Monograph of the Institute of Archaeology, Hebrew University of Jerusalem.

Braidwood, Robert J., and Bruce Howe

1960 *Prehistoric Investigations in Iraqi Kurdistan*. Studies in Ancient Oriental Civilization 31. Chicago: University of Chicago Press.

Dibble, Harold L.

1987 "The Interpretation of Middle Paleolithic Scraper Morphology." *American Antiquity* 52/1: 109–17.

1995 "Middle Paleolithic Scraper Reduction: Background, Clarification, and Review of the Evidence to Date." *Journal of Archaeological Method and Theory* 2/4: 299–368.

Downs, Elinor F., and Jerold M. Lowenstein

1995 "Identification of Archaeological Blood Proteins: A Cautionary Note." *Journal of Archaeological Science* 22/2: 11–16.

Eisele, J. A.; D. D. Fowler; G. Haynes; and R. A. Lewis

1995 "Survival and Detection of Blood Residues on Stone Tools." *Antiquity* 69: 36–46.

Garrod, Dorothy A. E.

1930 "The Palaeolithic of Southern Kurdistan: Excavations in the Caves of Zarzi and Hazar Merd." *Bulletin of the American School of Prehistoric Research* 6: 9–43.

Gobert, E.-G.

1950 "Le gisement paléolithique de Sidi Zin." *Karthago* 1: 1–38.

Hole, Frank, and Kent V. Flannery

1967 "The Prehistory of Southwestern Iran: A Preliminary Report." *Proceedings of the Prehistoric Society* 33: 147–206.

Hume, Gary W.

1976 "The Ladizian: An Industry of the Asian Chopper-chopping Tool Complex in Iranian Baluchistan." Philadelphia: Dorrance.

Lindly, John Michael

1997 The Zagros Mousterian: A Regional Perspective. Ph.D. dissertation, Arizona State University.

2005 *The Mousterian of the Zagros: A Regional Perspective*. Tempe: Arizona Board of Regents.

Loy, Thomas H.

1983 "Prehistoric Blood Residues: Detection on Tool Surfaces and Identification of Species of Origin." *Science* 220: 1269–71.

1985 "Blood Residue Analysis Identifies 100,000 Year Old Human Blood." *The Midden* 17/3: 7–8.

1992 "DNA and Proteins from Blood Residues on Stone Tools and Rock Art." Paper read at the Annual Meeting of the American Association for the Advancement of Science, Chicago, February 1992.

Newman, M., and P. Julig

1989 "The Identification of Protein Residues on Lithic Artifacts from a Stratified Boreal Forest Site." *Canadian Journal of Archaeology* 13: 119-32.

Newman, Margaret E.; Robert M. Yohe II; Howard Ceri; and Mark Q. Sutton

1993 "Immunological Protein Residue Analysis of Non-lithic Archaeological Materials." *Journal of Archaeological Science* 20/1: 93–100.

Sensabaugh, G. F.; A. C. Wilson; and P. L. Kirk

1971 "Protein Stability in Preserved Biological Remains: I. Survival of Biologically Active Proteins in an 8-year-old Sample of Dried Blood; II. Modification and Aggregation of Proteins in an 8-year-old Sample of Dried Blood." *International Journal of Biochemistry* 2/11: 545–68.

Shea, John J.

2013 *Stone Tools in the Paleolithic and Neolithic Near East: A Guide*. Cambridge: Cambridge University Press.

Solecki, Ralph S.

1971 *Shanidar: The First Flower People*. New York: Alfred A. Knopf.

Vaufrey, R.

1950 "La faune de Sidi Zin." *Karthago* 1: 40–64.

Wright, Herbert E., Jr.

1952 "Geologic Setting of Four Prehistoric Sites in Northeastern Iraq." *American Schools of Oriental Research Bulletin* 128: 11–24.

Wright, Herbert E., Jr., and Bruce Howe

1951 "Preliminary Report on Soundings at Barda Balka." *Sumer* 7: 107–18.

INTRODUCTION

HISTORY OF THE INVESTIGATIONS

The long-known Paleolithic site of Barda Balka ("standing stone," "stone to lean upon" in local Kurdish) is situated about 3 kilometers northeast of Chemchemal in Kirkuk Province, Iraq, at a point scarcely 200 meters southeast of the Kirkuk–Sulimaniyah highway, from which it is not easily visible (fig. 1). It lies at an elevation of about 740 meters above sea level on a hillside in the little hollow of a present-day minor dry-bed tributary of the Cham Shirwa Su, the principal axial stream of the Chemchemal Valley, which flows southeast to join the Basira Su and thence the Tauq Rivers. Until recent years, when it is rumored to have fallen down, the site has been conspicuously marked by a vertical, menhir-like, natural monolith of limestone conglomerate 3.5 meters high on a rather barren slope partly littered with Acheulean-type bifaces, pebble tools, cores, and flake artifacts (see pls. 1–4).

The site was discovered in 1949 by members of the Directorate General of Antiquities of Iraq while on archaeological reconnaissance in the district. Its significance was at once recognized, a sizeable surface collection was made of artifacts found on the slope of this little dry gully, and a brief note was published (al-Asil 1949).

In 1951, during a field season of the Oriental Institute of the University of Chicago under the direction of Robert J. Braidwood (which not only conducted the excavations at nearby Jarmo and Karim Shahir but also carried out wider geological and prehistoric reconnaissance in the extended Chemchemal Valley area), Barda Balka was again visited and further studied by Herbert E. Wright Jr. of the University of Minnesota Department of Geology and Bruce Howe, then of the Peabody Museum, Harvard University. At the gracious invitation of Dr. al-Asil, then director general of the Directorate of Antiquities and one of the discoverers of the site, it was arranged that small-scale soundings and geological studies should be made on behalf of the directorate to determine the type, age,

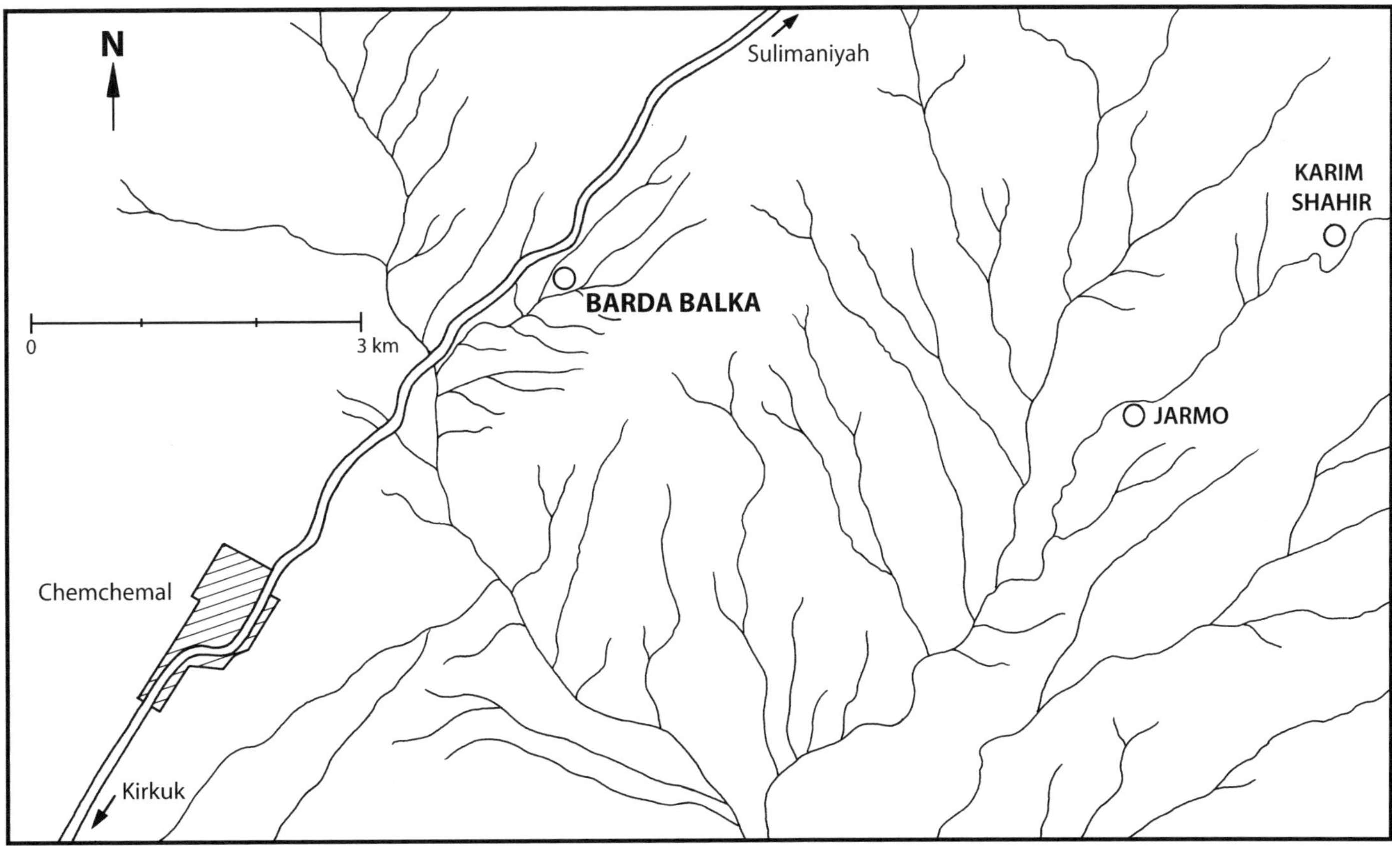

Figure 1. Location of Barda Balka north of Chemchemal along the Kirkuk–Sulimaniyah highway, Iraqi Kurdistan

and geological relationships of this prehistoric occupation site. Consequently, a four-day sounding campaign of trenching and localized geological investigations was promptly carried out (see pls. 1–2) and briefly reported on by Wright and Howe (1951).

GEOLOGICAL AND ARCHAEOLOGICAL RELATIONSHIPS

These efforts revealed that here, exposed near the base of a sizeable natural stratigraphic sequence, was a horizon containing an open-air workshop and animal-butchering site. These were centered on a spring (now inactive, its erstwhile underground channel is represented by the limestone conglomerate monolith) and on neighboring streamside beds of cobbles and pebbles and of finer gravels and sands (the stream is also long inactive, its deposits buried under massive subsequent sediments). Numerous pebble tools, bifaces, cores, various assorted flake tools, and trimming debris, along with a small quantity of poorly preserved animal bones, including some teeth, were all closely associated together with these deposits.

The stratigraphic sequence at Barda Balka continued upward from the pebble bed and gravel bed, with massive — essentially sterile — silt; and the whole aggradation sequence was subsequently dissected, truncating the aforementioned deposits and continuing downward to the level of the local present-day dry stream bed. On geological and geomorphological grounds, Wright (1952) considered that the pebble and gravel deposits containing this generally Middle Paleolithic occupation site might represent the start of an aggradation cycle, which comprised first the coarse pebble and gravel beds (resting on much older massive green clay) and then continued upward with the Jarmo Silts, the whole aggradation cycle representing the last local Pleistocene pluvial phase. This phase, by a further line of geological reasoning, might be correlated with the last Pleistocene glacial advance of Europe (Würm). The beginning of this period has been theoretically dated broadly to the time span of 60,000–100,000/120,000 years B.P. Thus, the same broad dating may be assigned to the Middle Paleolithic occupation site in the basal gravels of this aggradation cycle at Barda Balka (on dates, see *Foreword*).

The generous sample of the stone industry assembled from the deposits in the several sounding pits and from the surface at Barda Balka was given a preliminary field analysis and classification, and a representative typological cross section was deposited at the National Museum of Iraq in Baghdad (table 3). The remaining greater bulk of the assemblage was granted to the Oriental Institute of the University of Chicago, where it was subsequently studied by Howe. The stone industry described in this report is based on this latter body of material. The complete disposition of all the material of the stone industry from the 1951 campaign at Barda Balka is given below ("Artifacts from Barda Balka Deposited in Museums," p. 24).

The faunal remains from Barda Balka were studied, successively, by Fredrik Barth, then of the Ethnographic Museum of the University of Oslo; Dr. F. C. Fraser and Mr. Wilkins of the British Museum of Natural History; and Professor Charles A. Reed of the University of Illinois at Chicago. These studies are reported on below. In addition, the work of Thomas H. Loy, formerly of the British Columbia Provincial Museum, Canada, and then with the Department of Prehistory, Research School of Pacific Studies, Australia National University,[1] establishing traces of ancient blood on certain artifacts from the site, is also summarized below. No materials suitable for radioactive carbon determination were found.

[1] Thomas Loy died in 2005. — Ed.

THE EXCAVATIONS

In the very limited campaign of May 1951, nine exploratory trenches and pits were dug (fig. 2) near and at the monolith, and the stratigraphic and local geological relationships of the deposits were established. These were tentatively fitted into the broader geomorphological history constructed for the region by Wright (1952) and are considered at another point in this report.

The excavations and findings of the 1951 season are summarized below:

1. A discontinuous half-meter-wide trench (Trench 1) about 50 meters long and ranging from less than 1 to up to 2 meters in depth was dug from well down the slope, where artifacts littered the terrain of clay and shaley bedrock, directly uphill toward the summit, where easily dug reddish-buff calcareous silt lay under a light mantle of sparse vegetation. This trench revealed the stratigraphic sequence from the base upward (fig. 3):

    a. tilted shaley bedrock of Miocene age;

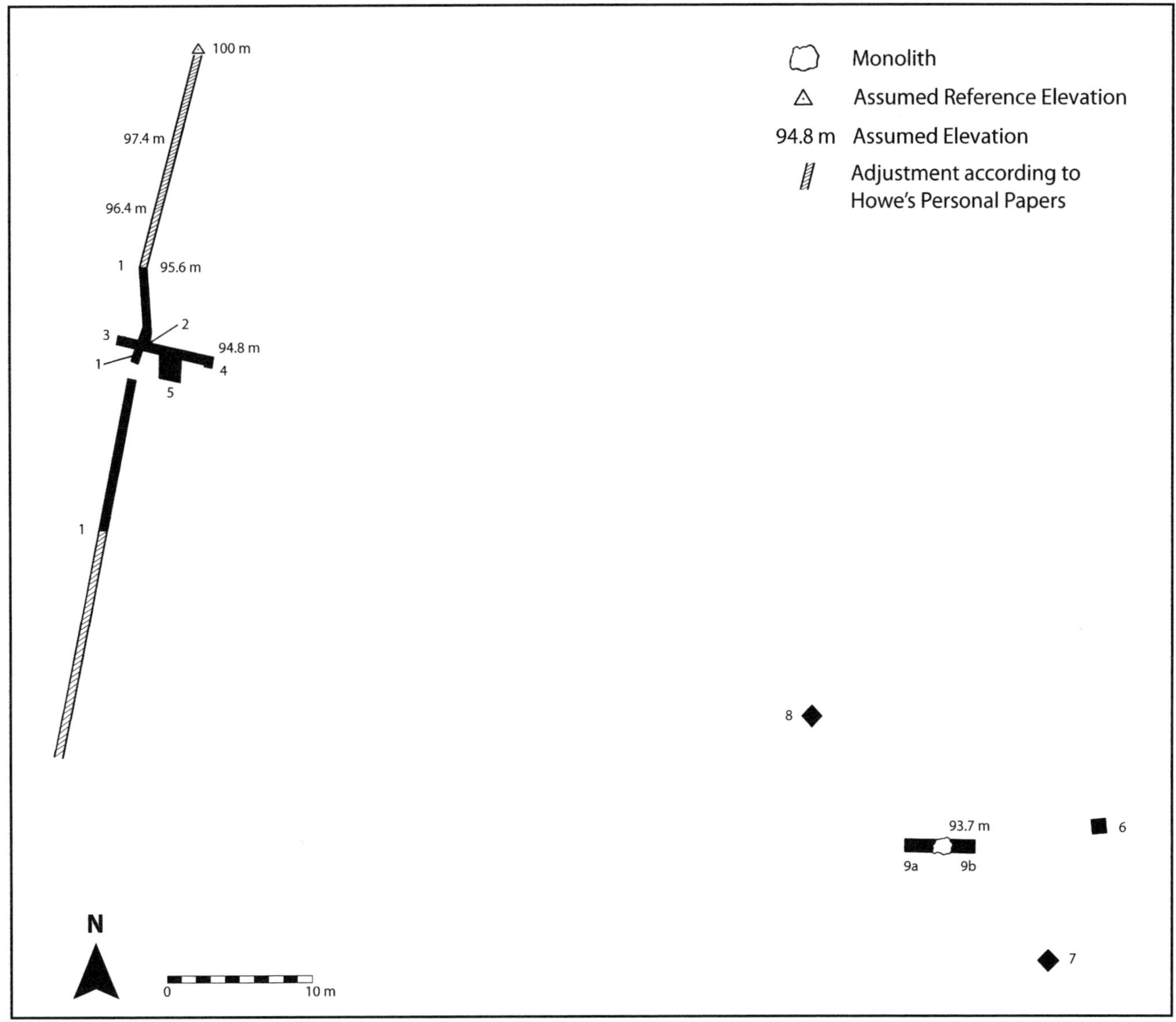

Figure 2. Plan of excavations, showing relation of trenches to monolith

b. about 5 meters of horizontally bedded, stiff, sterile green clay lying unconformably upon the tilted bedrock;

c. a conformable bed, 25–30 centimeters thick, of medium-size stream pebbles containing artifacts of the Lower/Middle Paleolithic occupation layer in situ (pl. 6; Trench 3);

d. a conformable layer, about 25 centimeters thick, of sterile, reddish-buff calcareous silt;

e. a conformable layer, about 30 centimeters thick, of sterile, green calcareous silt;

f. a conformable topmost layer of sterile, reddish-buff calcareous silts +3 meters thick.

2. Shallow extensions east and west of the long trench (Trench 1) were extended laterally at the level where it crossed and exposed the bed of stream pebbles containing some of the occupation site (Trench 2) so as to expose more of the occupation layer (Trenches 3, 4; pl. 6).

3. A trench 1.5 meters square (Trench 5) was dug 1 meter east of Trench 2 as a downslope extension of Trench 4. This was at the same level on the slope as the now just exposed stream pebble bed. This trench was established over the spot where a recent small-scale gravel exploitation had left a small raw depression. Dug to almost 1 meter depth, it disclosed smaller-size stream gravels and sands charged with quantities of stone artifacts. These included core, pebble, and many flake artifacts and smaller debris (possibly size-sorted along with the gravels by the stream action). Moreover, virtually all the limited faunal material found at this occupation site came from the gravels and sands of Trench 5.

4. Three other exploratory meter-square trenches (Trenches 6, 7, and 8) were dug at random points in the red silts and slopewash and were, respectively, a few meters east, south, and north of and at slightly lower or higher elevations than the occupation site, which was found in the pebble and gravel beds and within and about the base of the monolith. Each proved sterile and of no interest, and they have not been recorded further.

5. Finally, a half-meter-wide trench (Trench 9) was dug athwart the base of the nearby monolith to about 50 centimeters maximum depth on an east–west axis extending 2 meters out on the west side (Trench 9a) and 1.5 meters on the east (Trench 9b). This was in order to expose the base of the monolith and reveal its relationship to the surrounding deposits.

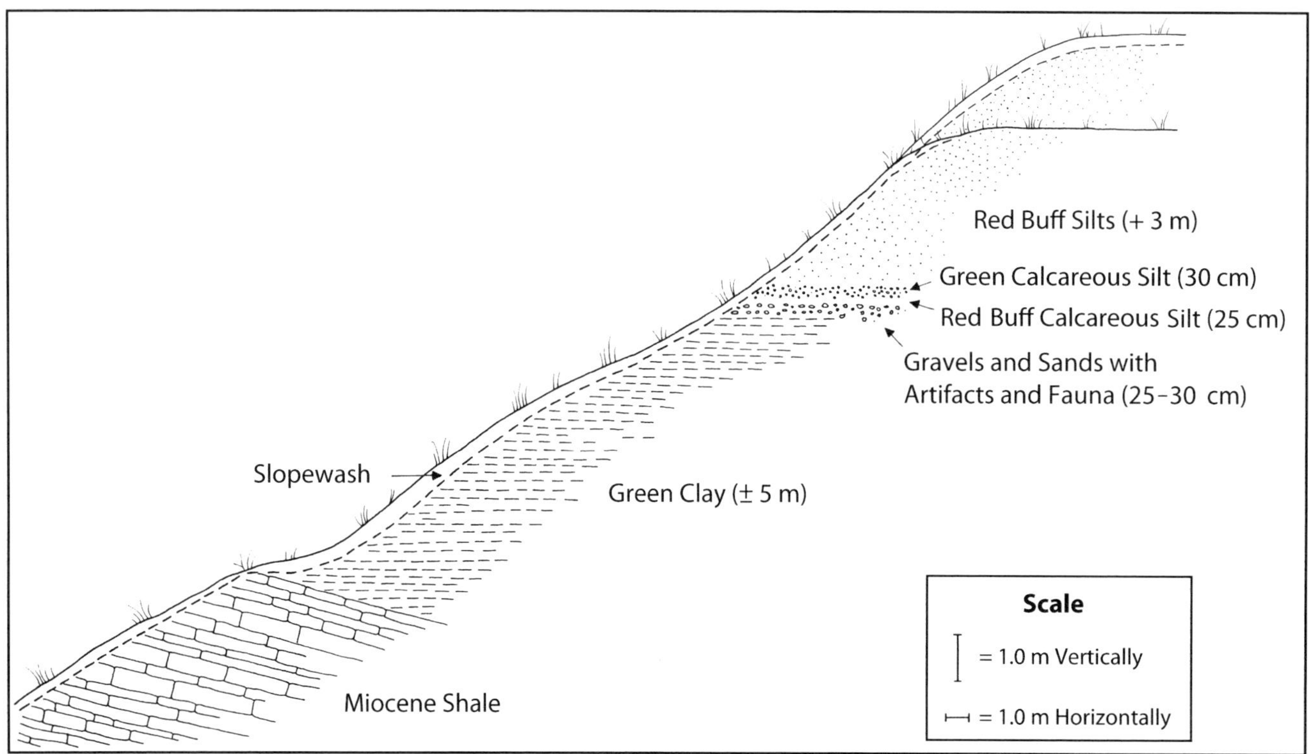

Figure 3. Schematic south–north section of deposits at Barda Balka

This excavation showed unequivocally that the freestanding monolith was a massive, firmly cemented, limestone conglomerate of sand, gravel, and pebbles with a few crisply flaked flint artifacts as well as bits of animal bones and teeth included and all markedly similar in size, condition, and composition to materials taken from the loose gravels, sands, and occupational debris in Trench 5 some 60 meters to the northwest. The above-ground portion of the standing stone passed uninterruptedly and integrally downward past the surrounding artifact-laden slope wash and into firmly consolidated gravelly deposits, essentially as a fully cemented column, although at the time of this excavation, it was distinctly beginning to erode and crumble away to a more narrow-waisted mass in the weathering zone just above and below the modern ground level (pls. 2–3). Boulder-sized blocks of this same conglomerate lay scattered widely just east and south of the monolith.

In the absence of a detailed contour map, the relative altitudes of the principal features at this hillside site were established by a series of barometric readings. These were made from a datum point set on the summit of the local massive red (Jarmo) silts shown at the top of the schematic section (fig. 3). There, an arbitrary altitude of 100 meters was fixed. Measuring downslope from this, relative altitudes were found for the following salient points:

1. General level of the exposed section of the occupation site (Trenches 1–5) = 94.8 m
2. Level of the visible base of the limestone conglomerate monolith (Trench 9) = 93.7 m
3. Level of the top of the monolith = 97.2 m

The levels of this limited exposed sector (Trenches 1–5) of a presumably wider occupation area and of the artifact-bearing ground-level portion of the spring core monolith are roughly the same. One may visualize the spring's active eye as having been conveniently to hand just above, at, or just below the stream-line level for the individuals of this streamside occupation site. The artifactual debris revealed as contained within the lower part of the monolith attests to this. The remaining 3.5-meters-high, freestanding mass of the monolithic core thrusts upward to well within the levels of the succeeding overlying sterile red Jarmo silts: the spring evidently outlived the time of the occupation horizon to a considerable degree, that is, to at least the level of the present-day top of the monolithic core.

Furthermore, the numerous conglomerate blocks littering the slope around the monolith hint at the weathering and break-up of a considerable surrounding area of calcareous spring deposit. Also, since these blocks and the spring-core monolith itself both contain traces of closely similar occupational debris, this suggests that living activities crowded in close around the spring, in effect expanding the extent of the occupational area some 60 meters farther east to include the spring area itself. One may thus assume at least a 70–80-meter frontage for this streamside occupation area truncated nowadays by the ground surface slope left by the modern erosion cycle. An immeasurable occupation area stretches back in behind this frontage, hidden under the overlying sedimentary deposits.

All the excavations were promptly and compactly filled in again before the brief investigation ended. The resulting picture allows one to reconstruct with some assurance a general history of the site and locality. In late Pleistocene and locally Middle Paleolithic times during the transition between the last interglacial and early last glacial stages, perhaps 60,000 to 100,000/120,000 years ago (on dates, see *Foreword* — Ed.), and probably in a climate somewhat like the present, a probably short-lived human occupation, devoted principally to stone working and tool making and evidently as well to animal butchering, was spread out over the pebble and gravel beds of this little side stream at a point centered about an active spring. This occupation site existed at the very start of a period of aggradation and was subsequently covered by 5 meters of further deposits of greenish and then reddish-buff silts, the greenish silts denoting a marshy phase. This aggradation cycle (representing all of the last glacial stage locally) ended and, thenceforward to the present, radical dissection and downcutting of the local landscape took over. The spring dried up, leaving its fossil core. The dissecting drainage regime progressively truncated the occupation site on the hillside along with the silts, gravels, pebbles, clay beds, and bedrock in this little tributary gully and also left 3.5 meters of the cemented spring core exposed as the monolith of the present time. Virtually all the archaeological surface material now to be found at the site is disposed downslope from the level on the hillside where the pebble and gravel beds containing a portion of the occupation site were truncated, exposed, and partly eroded away by the downcutting stream action and surface erosion.

DESCRIPTION OF THE STONE INDUSTRY

GENERAL

The jumbled and unsorted condition of the gravel deposit and of the nearby pebble bed makes detection of any stratification or sequence of occupations impossible. If indeed there had at any time been any succession of distinct layers or occupation horizons, they had disappeared by the time of the silt covering. What has been uncovered appears as one horizon: an assemblage evidently representing the remains of one or several closely recurrent temporary occupations set upon a dry portion of a stream bed clogged with a wide range of sands, gravels, pebbles, and cobbles. The concentration of stone and bone debris suggests that one sees this assemblage close to, if not actually in, its original position with, perhaps, some letting down or telescoping together by local erosion and deflation of fine-grain deposits of the several theoretically possible essentially coeval little occupations into one occupation layer.

The stone industry here appears to be of a single general time period and working tradition despite a little evidence to the contrary. On very few pieces (roughly 0.13%), double patination and comparatively fresh-looking secondary edge flaking at first suggest the possibility of two or more periods of occupation or at least reuse. However, the evidence is so little in quantity and sporadic in occurrence as to reduce the matter to insignificance. On the other hand, there is an outstanding phenomenon that may at first mislead the observer into supposing that there were multiple instances of occupation and fabrication. This is the coexistence at this site of the following:

1. bifaces almost exclusively of hard flint or chert, virtually all fresh and unworn looking;
2. many pebble tools predominantly of softer limestone or marble, some looking weathered and rolled, some fresh, some both;
3. many irregular, small, poorly made flake tools, mainly of flint, although a few limestone examples occur, mostly fresh and crisp looking.

Aside from the typological diversity represented here, it was clear that the limestone was softer, weaker, and more subject to weathering than the hard siliceous flint and chert. This characteristic in numerous cases gave it the appearance of being duller and more rolled and worn. This misleading innate character of the limestone was confirmed by a limited test carried out during the excavations. The position of limestone pieces in situ was carefully noted in an attempt to determine which face was weathered, if at all; and a number of pieces were marked in situ to show which portion lay facing upward. It was seen that the majority of these showed a dulled, leached, chalky, and often pitted or scoured surface on this upper side. On the underside, flake scars appeared relatively fresh and sharp and were darker and closer to the original rock color. Also, a limited coating of sand- and gravel-bearing calcareous crust was preserved on many of these lower faces. Apparently carbonates leached from above were precipitated on the underside of the artifacts, where water remained longer and evaporated more slowly, to produce a type of caliche. The chalky, silty, residual grainy, nubbly quality of the upper faces of the limestone became even clearer when the specimens were cleaned in the laboratory. The flake scar crests were also clearer than in the field: dulled on the upper, exposed faces and sharp on the under, sheltered faces. Reviewing the total assemblage, one found both pebble tools and a few bifaces of limestone with dulled scar ridges on one face and fresh ones on the opposite one. On the whole, the flint artifacts, not subject to such weathering, were remarkably fresh and unrolled looking. Both sorts may consequently be considered contemporaneous.

Stream-worn cobbles of flint or rarely limestone, flint breccia, or metamorphic rock (and one instance of a biface of basalt) were the source material for bifaces and flake tools, whereas stream-worn cobbles and pebbles of limestone and rarely marble were chosen for the making of pebble tools. All were presumably selected from the variegated torrential stream-bed materials lying in the many tributary gulleys and valleys of the surrounding landscape, ultimately derived as erosion products out of the higher ridges and hinterland of the foothills.

Thus, to summarize, the stone industry was made up of three general artifact categories — pebble tools, core bifaces, and flake tools — and was found in situ in the gravel and pebble beds along with poorly preserved and fragmentary animal bones and teeth, including some split and shattered long-bone fragments. The presence of ancient blood has recently been confirmed on certain flint artifacts. The evidence of double patinations was shown to be minimal and essentially insignificant. The evidence for rolling and wear on the lithic materials also appeared to be minimal and attributable almost exclusively to the differential weathering qualities of the soft limestone and marble employed. Consequently, one may conclude that this assemblage represents one industrial tradition. It was produced during one principal, or perhaps several briefer but more closely contemporary transient occupations, during one period of unknown length, at one site. Barda Balka was probably a small-scale combined workshop and animal-butchering site.

PEBBLE TOOLS

GENERAL

The excavators noted at the points dug in 1951 that the group of limestone pebble tools, as found in situ in the gravel and pebble beds, greatly outnumbered the bifaces, or bifacially flaked core tool group made on flint, although the latter constituted a relatively larger group in surface collections from the turf-covered slopes at Barda Balka. The source for the limestone pebbles was clearly the nearby stream beds marked by great quantities of stream-worn pebbles and cobbles of limestone and other rock. In the predominantly gravelly pit (Trench 5), eighty assorted pebble tools and five bifaces were found; in the adjoining, much more shallow and predominantly pebbly or cobbley portion of the same horizon (Trenches 2, 3, 4), thirty-six pebble tools and seven bifaces occurred. Likewise, in the combined lots of derived cumulative slopewash deposits in the various test pits (Trenches 6, 7, 8, 9) and trial Trench 1, a total of thirty-nine pebble tools and three bifaces turned up. In the surface collection conducted during the 1951 soundings, fifty-three pebble tools and thirty-five bifaces were found during several intensive searches. This surface sampling could be considered a less reliable or controlled indication of the true relative quantities of pebble and bifacial core tools than those from the limited in situ positions, as noted above. Results from surface collecting can be questionable because of the random and largely subjective nature of the activity. In addition, it is hard when done on a terrain masked by turf and other low growth. Finally, it is especially difficult under conditions where strikingly artificial large flint bifaces are perhaps more apparent than the largely natural-looking and inconspicuously flaked, less complex artifacts, made on limestone stream pebbles; and, by the same token, the smaller, flatter flake tools also catch the eye much less. Yet, allowance made for all these considerations, pebble tools still outnumbered bifaces at Barda Balka.

The pebbles on which these biface and pebble artifacts were made ranged in maximum dimensions from 12–15 centimeters to 4–5 centimeters. On some of the limestone pieces, a glossy sheen occurred in discontinuous isolated patches on the cortex surface, perhaps due to water and sand action in the stream bed. It appeared to bear no obvious or logical relation to artificial wear or use and could be observed on unused natural pebbles as well.

The 197 pebble tools found in situ have been classified into a number of subdivisions based on method of preparation or flaking. This classification was then also extended to the rest of the derived and surface specimens. The actual uses of these different types are unknown, despite the application of convenient and traditional tool names in some cases. Where certain rare, large limestone flakes have been worked into the same shapes and tool types as the simple pebble tools, they have been included with the latter. In general, secondary edge wear or flaking was not conspicuous or particularly developed, although it was present in numerous cases.

TYPOLOGICAL CLASSIFICATION

Truncated Pebbles

In Situ		*Combined Derived Slopewash*	*1951 Surface Collection*	**Total**
Pebble Bed	*Gravel Bed*			
4	9	4	4	**21**

A number of pieces were pebbles or pebble butts with flaked or broken faces almost perpendicular to the long axis and plane of the pebble mass extending usually straight across the narrow dimension (pl. 7:1–2). Only in rare instances do the flake scars along this truncation appear to be conchoidal and to have been from blows struck from one of the pebble faces, in the manner of the other retouched pebble tools. Rather, this truncating line appeared to be made up of relatively few stepped and flat or rarely somewhat convex-surfaced scars of the sort one might expect when a pebble is simply broken or smashed in two or used as a hammerstone. These pieces may have been the initial debris resulting from the preparation of such other more purposefully flaked pebble tools as were made on the matching half portions of these broken pebbles: they certainly had a different method of shaping (whether for further direct use or as a by-product), displaying random irregularly placed flat and amorphous flake scars.

Pebbles with 1–2 Flakes Removed from One End

In Situ		*Combined Derived Slopewash*	*1951 Surface Collection*	**Total**
Pebble Bed	*Gravel Bed*			
3	13	2	—	**18**

This group of elongated or discoid pebbles has had only one or two flakes removed at a relatively shallow angle from one face at one end and probably does not constitute a tool category. They may be either accidental products or else incipient artifacts too rudimentary and generalized to classify further.

Choppers: Simple Pebble Scrapers

In Situ		*Combined Derived Slopewash*	*1951 Surface Collection*	**Total**
Pebble Bed	*Gravel Bed*			
6	13	5	7	**31**

These artifacts consist of pebbles truncated transversely by steeply angled conchoidal flaking on one face from one direction on a diagonal or, more rarely, a direct straight line usually across the narrow dimension of the pebble (pl. 7:3). The working edge of these transversely and unifacially flaked pieces usually slopes either left or right. They slightly outnumber those with flaking extending straight across. This group forms a continuum with the next group, convex pebble scrapers flaked into half or three-quarter arcs.

Choppers: Convex Pebble Scrapers

	In Situ		*Combined Derived Slopewash*	*1951 Surface Collection*	**Total**
	Pebble Bed	*Gravel Bed*			
1/2 Arc	2	9	7	7	**25**
3/4 Arc	3	5	6	12	**26**
Total	**5**	**14**	**13**	**19**	**51**

This group consists predominantly of pebble portions or halves that have been flaked at a steep angle from one direction on one face across the narrow dimension into a convex working edge with the unifacial flaking extending either in a gentle arc simply across the width of the pebble (pl. 7:4) or in a more pronounced arc along two-thirds or three-fourths of the circumference of the piece. The former, less extended variety is only slightly outnumbered by the latter, and both form a continuum with the foregoing simple scrapers, being set off only by the outline and extent of their flaked edges. A few have been made on large, bulky flakes (one from slopewash deposits, four from the surface).

Choppers: Pointed or Spatulate Pebble Tools

	In Situ		*Combined*	*1951*	**Total**
	Pebble Bed	*Gravel Bed*	*Derived Slopewash*	*Surface Collection*	
Pointed	2	5	—	5	**12**
Spatulate	4	5	2	4	**15**
Total	**6**	**10**	**2**	**9**	**27**

This group consists of pebbles that have been unifacially flaked at a shallow angle, producing invasive flake scars over a considerable area of that face. This flaked area produces either a broad, spatulate edge in a majority of cases (pl. 7:5–6) or a diagonally tapering pointed edge resembling the outline of bifaces or bifacially flaked core tools (pl. 7:7). Not only do some have the shape and extensive flaking at the point end, but one or two also have isolated flaking on two faces, one even having alternate opposite-edge flaking. Indeed, certain specimens of these choppers suggest, by the wider extent of their flaking, that some of this group may be a stage in the manufacture of pebble-butted or other core bifaces, were it not for the fact that virtually all of the biface category is of flint and that the pebble chopper group is exclusively of limestone. In this group, a number are made on thick flakes with either the cortex face or the flake-scar face being worked (one in situ from the pebble bed; three from the surface).

Chopping Tools: Bifacially Flaked Pebble Tools

In Situ		*Combined*	*1951*	**Total**
Pebble Bed	*Gravel Bed*	*Derived Slopewash*	*Surface Collection*	
3	10	7	9	**29**

The majority of pieces in this group are elongated pebbles with one or more flake scars on each of two opposing faces at one narrow end (pl. 8:1). A few have this bifacially worked edge along one long dimension set either straight or diagonally (pl. 8:2). Another few have this on a tapering or pointed end in a manner approaching that of the biface or "handax," but are much less complex in preparation, the pebble cortex portion representing over two-thirds of the total surface and the flaked portion being confined to one extreme edge or end zone.

Bipolar: Two-ended Pebble Tools

In Situ		*Combined*	*1951*	**Total**
Pebble Bed	*Gravel Bed*	*Derived Slopewash*	*Surface Collection*	
5	7	1	5	**18**

A few pebbles were found that had one or more flakes knocked off each opposing narrow end (pl. 8:3–5). The majority of cases showed flaking on one face only, though a few bore flaking on two, or alternate opposite faces. One specimen in the pebble bed and one on the surface bore flaking not primarily at the narrow ends but along the two opposing long edges on both faces. The set of the flaking may be steep or else low angled and shallow, and the worked edges produced by it may be variously sharp or blunted, straight or diagonal, spatulate and convex, or pointed.

On the whole, this does not suggest a complex tool type since only a few flakes have been removed, although there are enough flakes to suggest it is not fortuitous or natural. It may be an intermediate bit-tool with flakes knocked off by indirect percussion, a chisel form; or else a sinker with flakes removed to form a depression to facilitate hafting.

Flaked Polyhedral Spheres, or "Boules"

In Situ		*Combined Derived Slopewash*	*1951 Surface Collection*	***Total***
Pebble Bed	*Gravel Bed*			
—	—	2	—	**2**

No specimens of this type were found in situ, but two occurred in derived slopewash deposits and have the same physical appearance as the material coming from the pebble and gravel beds. Both are of limestone and were flaked roughly so as to form a crude, facetted sphere the size of a tennis ball (pl. 9:1). One piece retained considerable pebble cortex, its area already well rounded in nature, and measured about 8 × 8 × 8 centimeters. The other measured about 6.5 × 6.5 × 6.5 centimeters and was flaked on all sides.

CORE BIFACE IMPLEMENTS

GENERAL AND TYPOLOGICAL CLASSIFICATION

Flaked core-derived implements at Barda Balka, including predominantly bifaces or "handaxes" and one or two other isolated forms, are virtually all made of chert or flint breccia of varying but generally poor quality, with a very few notable exceptions that are made on limestone or igneous rock (pls. 9–12, 16). Again, the obvious immediate source was the stream-worn pebbles of like materials close at hand in the stream beds of the valley. With one exception, specimens of every type as well as all illustrated examples here were found in situ in either the pebble bed or the gravel bed. Many biface or "handax" specimens retain pebble cortex on one or both faces or at the butt (pl. 9:2–3). A number were made on large flakes, as their partly effaced bulbar flake-scar face or plano-convex cross section betrayed (pl. 10:1).

The overall surface flaking used to shape the artifacts in this whole category consists of broad, irregular, invasive flakes that are usually shallow to nearly flat, but also in some cases more concave and deeply cut. This suggests, respectively, bone- or wood-on-stone and stone-on-stone techniques. In addition, there is often further secondary edge flaking of stepped or flatter sorts helping to make straighter, less sinuous working edges.

The outline shapes range from occasionally cordiform (pl. 10:1) to commonly pear shaped or almond shaped, the rounded butts being generally broad and thick, some with pebble cortex butts, and the points either broad and obtuse or, more often, narrow and acute (pl. 10:2–3). Only one debatable example of a biface approaching the classic narrow elongated "Micoquean" type of pointed biface was found (pl. 11:1), but this lacked the very attenuated point and swollen, bulky, rounded butt-end combination of the exaggerated classic form.

Concerning other possible forms, very occasionally (three surface specimens and two in situ), a core- or large flake-piece will show a preponderance of work or wear along one long edge and a blunted or thick-proportioned, deliberately flaked zone along the opposite long edge, suggesting broad-fronted cleavers. These might be either single-edge scrapers with thick-butted backs or else double scrapers with a thick steep-fronted scraper-like edge and an opposite, thinner, knife-like working edge. However, these are not a significant common type here. Certain other large flakes or fragments have a roughly rhomboidal cross section and bear flaking on one or both faces.

One such piece requires further description. It was made on dark gray basalt, appeared somewhat rolled, and came from the surface east of the monolith. Its natural source is presumably the same stream gravels as that postulated for the rest of the assemblage. The physical state and techno-typological features of the artifact conform fully with the in situ materials. It has a coarsely flaked butt at one narrow end and a large flake removed transversely across each face at the opposite narrow tip end to form a broad sharp cutting edge in the classic form of a cleaver, or "hachereau" (pl. 11:2). Finally, a single chert specimen of trihedral pick-like form with thick triangular cross section was found in situ in the gravel bed. This artifact is illustrated (Wright and Howe 1951, fig. 2; Braidwood and Howe 1960, pl. 26:1), but being typologically unique in the assemblage, it not only has been included in the selection deposited at the National Museum of Iraq, but has also been counted here.

Table 1. Core biface implements

Type	*In Situ*		*Combined Derived Slopewash*	*1951 Surface Collection*	***Total***
	Pebble Bed	*Gravel Bed*			
Cordiform	—	—	1	6	**7**
Pear or Almond Shaped	1	1	1	10	**13**
Pebble Butted	3	—	1	8	**12**
On Flakes	1	2	—	8	**11**
"Micoquean"	1	—	—	—	**1**
Cleaver	—	2	—	3	**5**
Trihedral	—	1	—	—	**1**
Truncated Fragments, Unclassifiable	—	—	1	6	7
Total	**6**	**6**	**4**	**41**	**57**

LARGE FLAKES, PERHAPS USED AS SCRAPERS

In Situ		*Combined Derived Slopewash*	*1951 Surface Collection*	***Total***
Pebble Bed	*Gravel Bed*			
5	13	2	9	**29**

A number of large, shapely flakes of chert or limestone have poor stepped retouch or wear, in varying degrees, along one relatively thin, long edge or, rarely, across their narrow end like a cleaver, or "hachereau." The use may be well developed or quite rudimentary. The profile outline of this edge may be convex or concave in one or several zones. Often the opposite long edge is thicker and steep-fronted, less flaked, and is serviceable as a grip or butt.

Sizes range from 19 × 12 centimeters maximum (one example) down through common sizes of 12 × 8 and 10 × 7 centimeters to 7 × 4 and 6 × 5 centimeters. By virtue of their particular specific zones of edge flaking, these last smallest specimens are placed arbitrarily in this category of well-formed flakes, as opposed to the many examples grouped in the more general irregular used flake implement division dealt with below ("Used Flakes, Bladelike Flakes, and Fragments," p. 20). Quite a number are the primary or secondary flakes off a pebble, carrying off the cortex or cortex-and-flake scars on one face.

FLAKE IMPLEMENTS

GENERAL

The outstanding characteristics of the flake component of the Barda Balka assemblage are the crudeness, irregularity, and simplicity of pieces, as well as the quantity, which exceeds that of the other major categories. It is also virtually all of flint or chert with only very few pieces being of limestone or other materials. It should be noted, too, that the great majority of pieces came from the gravel bed with its characteristically medium- to smaller-size elements and that very few came from the bed of grosser pebbles and cobbles close by. Moreover, the significant edge flaking found on much of this flake category, whether by re-touch or use, is distinctly concentrated and developed to a degree beyond the desultory flaking noted on pieces of ordinary debris that otherwise perhaps show only the usual amount of scattered natural edge attrition flaking at an open-air site such as Barda Balka.

Side scrapers and hollow scrapers, or notched flakes, are the two most numerous and characteristic subclasses, the one in general merging typologically into the other. Although certain rough recurrent regularities of outline form suggest that many specimens of each type were deliberately so struck or prepared, or at least deliberately chosen for pre-existing shapes and the set of angles that they had, there is also a great proportion that seems obviously to have been produced simply by wear on numerous miscellaneous pieces, the worn edges or concavities developing at selected points as they were used. A few cases of combination side and hollow scrapers occur, but, generally, a given piece displays one form or the other.

In addition to these two distinct tool types, there are what might be termed discoid or rounded scrapers, formed by wear or limited preparation on a convex edge of irregular flakes and fragments. Next, an exceptional few similarly developed pieces resemble end scrapers or steep scrapers, being on either the narrow dimension of elongated pieces or else the bulkier front of thick pieces, respectively. Flakes and fragments with alternate opposite-edge retouch or wear form a small group that may be viewed as a continuum with certain of the notched flakes noted above. The remainder of this large subdivision of flake artifacts is composed of only somewhat used and worn flakes and fragments of all sizes and shapes, although some bear quite heavy nicking and batter.

The few blades and bladelike flakes found were so rare as to be considered fortuitous and not a true part of the techno-typology here. The proportion of facetted to unfacetted striking platforms, among the pieces where this feature was observable, is somewhat less than 40 percent in general. A few core revival tablets and flakes were found but are not a distinctive feature at the site. Core forms from which all the aforementioned flake artifacts were presumably derived are medium- to small-size discoids, numerous irregular pebble cores, and rare polyhedral or amorphous forms and are treated separately below.

The occurrence of double patina on some pieces at first raised the possibility of two periods of use or manufacture. However, the number of cases was so rare and the patination confined to so limited a zone of edge flaking that it may be considered negligible and reasonably attributable to isolated instances of very limited possible brief and haphazard reuse or to accidental flaking. The instances of double patination found on pieces in the shallow pebble bed, which lay relatively near the surface in the area dug, was in general more advanced and ochreous than the examples of double patination in the deeper, more protected gravel bed where these instances were either milky or non-existent. Thus, this phenomenon of double patination appears likely to have been a development in situ limited to association with the pebbly and gravelly stream bed and its various natural circumstances.

TYPOLOGICAL CLASSIFICATION

Side Scrapers

On Flakes with End Blow: Pebble Cortex Back

		In Situ		*Combined Derived Slopewash*	*1951 Surface Collection*	***Total***
		Pebble Bed	*Gravel Bed*			
Unworked Striking Platform	*Obverse Worked*	2	36	—	—	**38**
	Reverse Worked	1	13	—	—	**14**
Facetted Striking Platform	*Obverse Worked*	—	9	—	—	**9**
	Reverse Worked	—	—	—	—	—
Total		**3**	**58**	—	—	**61**

Examples on flakes with end blow with pebble cortex back is the largest and most distinct sub-group among side scrapers. This sub-group consists of elongate irregular primary flakes perhaps either purposefully struck off or else selected for their preexisting thicker edge and pebble cortex remnant. This edge and side was left unworked while the thin, sharp, opposite, long flake edge was developed into the single scraping edge. The great majority of these flakes have unfacetted striking platforms and have their edge flaking on the obverse, or non-bulbar, face (pl. 12:1–5).

In virtually all cases, the retouch or wear along the single predominantly used edge is a combination of invasive irregular squamous flaking and the stepped variety commonly associated with Mousterian-type side scrapers. In a few individual cases, the flaking is not invasive but approaches a narrow steep edge retouch that follows the sinuous flake edge. Lengths range from a few at 8–10 centimeters, through a majority at 5–6 centimeters, down to small ones at 3–4 centimeters, and one that is 2 centimeters long.

On Flakes with End Blow: Two Edges Converging to a Point

	In Situ		*Combined Derived Slopewash*	*1951 Surface Collection*	***Total***
	Pebble Bed	*Gravel Bed*			
Unworked Striking Platform	4	15	—	—	**19**
Facetted Striking Platform	—	10	—	—	**10**
Total	**4**	**25**	—	—	**29**

This sub-group is on triangular flakes, although some few are rhomboidal. These might be confused with so-called points but for their unbalanced irregular asymmetric form, the thick conformation of most pieces, and the central placement of the edge flaking that does not always run equally to the very tips on either or both edges. All this suggests that they are more reasonably viewed as scrapers. The flaking is generally as noted in the section above and may occur entirely on one face or, occasionally, on alternate opposite faces. One edge is generally the predominantly worked one with stepped and squamous scars, while the other edge bears less developed and more steep or nibbled scars, if any. This circumstance of asymmetric features argues strongly for use as some sort of scraping or cutting tool rather than for a balanced symmetric projectile point. A few cases of two edges with equally developed work occur (pl. 12:6–9). The sizes range from a very few with a maximum length of 6–7 centimeters, through a majority at 4.0–5.5 centimeters, down to a few at 2.5–3.0 centimeters long.

On Flakes with End Blow: Irregular Flakes — Elongate, Oval, and Merging into Triangular

	In Situ		*Combined Derived Slopewash*	*1951 Surface Collection*	**Total**
	Pebble Bed	*Gravel Bed*			
Unworked Striking Platform	1	21	—	—	**22**
Facetted Striking Platform	3	5	—	—	**8**
Total	**4**	**26**	—	—	**30**

Various irregularly shaped specimens not bearing pebble cortex backs and not involving the triangular outline form with converging worked edges belong in this category. They may be worked on one or both long edges and faces, but predominently one edge of the obverse, or non-bulbar, face is the one so marked (pl. 12:10–17). Sizes range from 6–7 centimeters through 4–5 centimeters maximum length, composing the bulk of examples, down to a few 2–3 centimeters maximum dimension. On the whole, these are small-sized artifacts.

On Flakes with Side Blow: Pebble Cortex Back

	In Situ		*Combined Derived Slopewash*	*1951 Surface Collection*	**Total**
	Pebble Bed	*Gravel Bed*			
Unworked Striking Platform	—	6	—	—	**6**
Facetted Striking Platform	—	4	—	—	**4**
Total	—	**10**	—	—	**10**

This group of primary flakes has the same characteristics in general as the end-blow category, but there are no large specimens, 4.0–4.5 centimeters being the maximum dimensions of the largest specimen. These are marked by steep working fronts and by thick cortex butts or backs.

On Flakes with Side Blow: Two Edges Converging to a Point

	In Situ		*Combined Derived Slopewash*	*1951 Surface Collection*	**Total**
	Pebble Bed	*Gravel Bed*			
Unworked Striking Platform	—	1	—	—	**1**
Facetted Striking Platform	1	—	—	—	**1**
Total	**1**	**1**	—	—	**2**

There are only two medium-small specimens of asymmetric points, one with poorly developed edge work on both converging edges, the other well retouched. Dimensions are 3.5 × 3.5 and 2.5 × 4.0 centimeters, respectively.

On Flakes with Side Blow: Irregular Flakes — Elongate, Oval, and Merging into Triangular

	In Situ		*Combined Derived Slopewash*	*1951 Surface Collection*	**Total**
	Pebble Bed	*Gravel Bed*			
Unworked Striking Platform	1	7	—	—	**8**
Facetted Striking Platform	2	5	—	—	**7**
Total	**3**	**12**	—	—	**15**

Again, this is a small group of virtually all small specimens having 2.5 × 3.5 centimeters as maximum dimensions, although two are 4.5–5.0 centimeters maximum and one is 6 centimeters long. Edge flaking features are the same as on their end-blow flake counterparts above: one or both long edges and faces may display stepped, squamous, steep, or nibbled flaking, denoting differing activities.

On Fragments: Pebble Cortex Back

In Situ		*Combined Derived Slopewash*	*1951 Surface Collection*	***Total***
Pebble Bed	*Gravel Bed*			
2	14	—	—	**16**

Fragments are either portions of larger pieces or of flakes whose bulb is not discernible. Many of the pieces in this sub-group are thickly triangular in cross section and have a steep working face. One specimen from the pebble bed is worked along nearly two-thirds of its edge and has working zones that may be viewed as a combination of (1) side scraper, (2) convex and/or discoid scraper, and (3) concave and/or hollow scraper. Sizes range from 5–7 centimeters down to a few at 3.5–4.0 centimeters in length and one with 2.5 centimeters as maximum dimension. Typologically this is not a very important group.

On Fragments: Triangular Fragments Converging to a Point

In Situ		*Combined Derived Slopewash*	*1951 Surface Collection*	***Total***
Pebble Bed	*Gravel Bed*			
1	6	—	—	**7**

Included here are steep thick triangular-sectioned pieces of sharp acute triangular or flat obtuse triangular outline that bear flaking on alternate opposite faces. Sizes range from 4.5 centimeters (a broken piece probably originally larger) down to 2.5–3.0 centimeters maximum dimensions.

On Fragments: Irregular Fragments

In Situ		*Combined Derived Slopewash*	*1951 Surface Collection*	***Total***
Pebble Bed	*Gravel Bed*			
6	31	—	—	**37**

These are highly irregularly shaped and often thick pieces producing stubby medium to small scrapers with steep working fronts variously placed on the piece.

On Fragments: Fragments of Scrapers too Small to Classify

In Situ		*Combined Derived Slopewash*	*1951 Surface Collection*	***Total***
Pebble Bed	*Gravel Bed*			
12	70	—	—	**82**

These small fragments all had the steep faces, or shallow narrow faces, bearing stepped or squamous edge flaking characteristic of the whole group of side scrapers described above.

General Remarks on Patinas and Striking Platforms

No trace of any double patina was found on any of the side scrapers. Regarding the presence of facetted or unfacetted striking platforms on the scraper specimens where observable, the following different occurrences were tallied:

Unworked Wide Angle	31	30%
Unworked Normal Angle	50	48%
Facetted	23	22%
Total	**104**	**100%**

Rounded Scrapers

	In Situ		*Combined Derived Slopewash*	*1951 Surface Collection*	***Total***
	Pebble Bed	*Gravel Bed*			
Unworked Striking Platform	8	11	–	–	**19**
Facetted Striking Platform	4	2	–	–	**6**
Unclassifiable Fragments	3	15	–	–	**18**
Total	**15**	**28**	**–**	**–**	**43**

Rounded scrapers is a group that, although a few specimens display a limited zone of what may be taken as deliberate edge retouch, comprises mostly pieces that appear to have developed by use rather than preparation. Whichever the case, the artifacts have in common the great irregularity of the flakes or fragments employed and one convex edge front sector that has been used as, or made into, a convex scraping edge. With the exception of eleven steep-fronted, plano-convex thick pieces, all the rest are on relatively thin flat flakes or fragments. The great majority are on small pieces and resemble thumbnail scrapers in size and dimensions; another eight pieces are medium-size broad flakes that have had one corner or a broad front rounded off into a convex scraper edge. Edge flaking ranges from stepped and squamous, especially on the steep high-fronted thick examples, to steep narrow flaking on the smaller pieces (pl. 13:1–5).

In two cases, both from the gravel bed, there was evidence of double patina, but this was only slightly contrasting. In each case, the piece is a small-size thumbnail-type scraper on a fragment of a flake whose original size and outline have been completely lost and, in all probability, much reduced to its present dimensions. The possibility is that the older, more patinated, slightly milky, yellower, more soiled or creamy central scar surfaces on both faces of both pieces represent the patination from the time they lay on the surface of the original working floor or stream bed. The younger, virtually unpatinated, lighter, and cleaner gray peripheral scar faces confined to the edge flaking probably date from the time of artifact production. There can be no question of their not being in situ, as calcareous gray greenish crust adhered to both pieces, and the inner mass of both has the typical gray color of the great majority of specimens in the gravel pit. The contrast in patination is so slight that the two periods need not to have been widely separated in time. One piece has a slightly rolled or dulled appearance on some scars. All in all, these two pieces were originally most likely found by the ancient flint knappers as flakes among streamside workshop debris and converted to implements.

Concave Scrapers/Notched Flakes Continuum

	In Situ		*Combined*	*1951*	**Total**
	Pebble Bed	*Gravel Bed*	*Derived Slopewash*	*Surface Collection*	
Irregular Flakes, Fragments	22	130	57	—	**209**
Bladelike Flakes, Fragments	1	20	—	—	**21**
One Central Notch on Flakes, Fragments	8	74	—	—	**82**
Steep, Plane-like Flakes, Fragments	11	87	—	—	**98**
Total	**42**	**311**	**57**	—	**410**

This large miscellaneous group, even more than the side-scraper group, is marked by the fact that the edge flaking on the artifacts seems due to wear and use rather than deliberate manufacture. There are two general sorts of pieces into which wide or small concavities (pl. 13:6–9) or notches (pl. 13:10–12) have been worked, either singly or in multiples: (a) irregular, generally broad and flat, but also small and stubby flakes, fragments, or bladelike flakes; and (b) elongated narrow or else thick irregular pieces with steep-fronted high cross section (pl. 13:13).

The former display notches or hollows anywhere along their thin edges on either face and resemble notched flakes; the latter have this hollow, more often broad and shallow than narrow and deep, developed along a long edge on a steep high front in the manner of a plane, or spoke-shave. A third possible variation, included with the irregular flakes and fragments, is one where the piece bears one major rather deep worn notch, or occasional twin or paired notches. These are flanked by two protruding unworked remnants, or horns. They may jut out either equally to make a roughly symmetric piece with centered notch, or else unequally to produce a notch with a set, or thrust, off to left or right. Some of these resemble the form of a concave end scraper, being on the narrow dimension of an elongated piece. Large specimens range up to 6–7 centimeters in maximum dimension, medium sizes 3.0–5.5 centimeters, and small ones below 3 centimeters. In observable cases, the relative quantities of facetted and plain unworked striking platforms (in those cases where enough of the striking platform can be observed to make a judgment) are given in the following table:

	Striking Platform		
	Unfacetted	*Facetted*	*Indeterminate*
Irregular Flakes, Fragments	27	18	94
Bladelike Flakes, Fragments	7	3	10
Total	**34**	**21**	**104**

Concerning double patinations, in the one sub-category where it occurs, "irregular flakes, fragments," three pieces, each with an obvious artificial bulb of percussion and striking platform, were found with such patination. These three instances were as follows:

1. blue-white patina over one face, honey colored to milky patina over the other except on edge-notching scars, where it was less advanced but still milky;
2. dead-white patina on one face cut into by large-size edge flaking of nearly fresh gray tone and on under face a dappled milky blue patina over the face including the edge notching;
3. slightly fresher gray and milkier white patina on flake-scar faces within a notch that cuts into the soiled yellow-drab patinated surface elsewhere on the piece.

Otherwise, the only other doubly patinated piece among 410 such artifacts was one of the steep-faced plane-like hollow scrapers. This was mainly milky gray but had, on the steep face of the hollow scraper, front edge-flaking scars of two shades of darker fresh gray with only a faint milky film. Thus, once again, double patinations are demonstrably insignificant at Barda Balka.

Steep Scrapers

In Situ		*Combined Derived Slopewash*	*1951 Surface Collection*	**Total**
Pebble Bed	*Gravel Bed*			
1	1	26	14	**42**

A rare type (also informally labeled "tea-cosy" scraper), this scraper form is elongated oval in plan and steeply pyramidal in cross section, has a flat smooth flake-scar underface, is irregularly flaked all around and over the obverse face, and has signs of relatively heavy edge wear mainly on the long edges rather than at the ends (pl. 13:13). Thus they cannot be labeled a nosed scraper; without concavities they cannot be hollow scrapers; nor, with their overall humped-up mass and their extensive rather uniform obverse bilateral edge flaking, can they be the usual side scrapers. Plan dimensions of these in situ specimens are 4.0 × 1.5 and 3.5 × 2.0 centimeters, respectively, the usual size and dimension range for this type elsewhere.

End Scrapers

In Situ		*Combined Derived Slopewash*	*1951 Surface Collection*	**Total**
Pebble Bed	*Gravel Bed*			
1	8	8	1	**18**

Flakes, bladelike flakes, and fragments, having an elongated overall shape and a narrow end with marked wear or flaking thereon, have been labeled end scrapers if the working edge is not concave enough to warrant inclusion with "hollow scrapers" or broadly convex enough to be put with "rounded scrapers." Most of the working scraper ends are straight or diagonal; six are convex ended. The type is relatively crude, not distinctive or plentiful. Only one example has been made on a true bladelike flake (pl. 13:14), and the rest are all on irregular flakes or fragments. With the exception of two of the convex-ended ones, evidently retouched with neater, more regular controlled edge flaking, all the rest seem due to wear. None has indications of double patina.

Flakes and Fragments with Steep Alternate-face Edge Retouch or Wear

In Situ		*Combined Derived Slopewash*	*1951 Surface Collection*	**Total**
Pebble Bed	*Gravel Bed*			
14	50	21	11	**96**

The pieces in this category lack sufficiently developed notches to be placed in the hollow scrapers/notched flakes continuum, but do have close-set, steep, small-scale squamous or deeply bitten flake scars set in unequal groups alternately on one face or the other around much or all of the circumference (pl. 13:15–16). In some cases it appears as if a plain or facetted striking platform might have existed but had been obliterated in the course of the subsequent edge flaking.

The majority of these pieces are small or medium (1.5–3.0 centimeters diameter), and only three pieces exceed these with maximum dimensions of 3.5–5.0 centimeters. No double patination was observed here, where, of all categories of used and reused amorphous pieces, it might have been expected.

This may not actually be a true implement type and may be merely the product of fortuitous pressures or attrition, by trampling, pounding, or re-deposition at a streamside workshop site. Nevertheless, its edge flaking resembles techno-typological features found with some regularity at other similarly early sites.

Used Flakes, Bladelike Flakes, and Fragments

In Situ		*Combined Derived Slopewash*	*1951 Surface Collection*	***Total***
Pebble Bed	*Gravel Bed*			
99	989	256	381	**1,725**

This larger group contains pieces with signs of edge wear or use or slight flaking remnants of work too rudimentary or limited to be included in any other category. It is a conglomeration of edge-flaked pieces of widely varying size and shape. While there is some heavy bifacial, deeply gouged nicking in cases, the greater bulk is marked by irregular, variously invasive squamous, steep, or rarely nibbled edge flaking. Some few limestone or marble specimens occur among the great variety of chert and flint.

Among the over thousand pieces in situ in the pebble bed and gravel bed, seven pieces displayed a faintly contrasting ochreous double patina. Among those flakes with observable striking platforms, plain unfacetted specimens were nearly twice as frequent as the facetted ones. Among the plain ones, the wide-angled ("Clacton") type was 57 percent of the whole, although the flakes were often small and delicate and not in the typically large and heavy "Clacton" style.

Trimming Flakes and Fragments

Miscellaneous flake pieces, mostly fragmentary, with no significant traces of edge flaking of any sort, remained after the classification into the various foregoing typological flake categories. Of the 1,689 such pieces, most came from the gravel bed. In the 143 observable cases, the striking platform was facetted in only a handful of cases, the majority being plain. Of these last, 61 percent had normal angles, 39 percent the wide-angle platform.

Flint Flake with Sheen

One unused flake has a tip and angle on one corner of its obverse face marked by a small zone of distinct and unmistakable sheen. This is highly shiny and clear in appearance. From the conformation of scar lines and the direction of flaking, it is clear that the sheen overlies part of one end of the striking platform. This piece was definitely in situ in the gravel bed, has the familiar concretion adhering, and is of the fresh two-tone ochreous and gray flint characteristic of this assemblage. The piece is unique among the material collected at Barda Balka. The sheen is too sharply defined and localized to be stream polish, which would surely be more widely spread on this piece and perhaps be more widely found on other pieces in the assemblage. A number of the limestone and marble pebble pieces display a shiny surface on their cortex suggesting stream polish, but the gloss was not otherwise found on any flint pieces. Thus at present there is no explanation for this single instance of sharply limited gloss.

CORES

	In Situ		*Combined Derived Slopewash*	*1951 Surface Collection*	***Total***
	Pebble Bed	*Gravel Bed*			
Discoid	7	30	2	17	**56**
Pebble	7	57	3	19	**86**
Polyhedral	1	9	1	1	**12**
Total	**15**	**96**	**6**	**37**	**154**
Miscellaneous Core Fragments	41	365	137	100	**643**

Three major types of cores occurred together in the assemblage at Barda Balka. These were as follows:

1. Discoid cores marked by radially disposed flaking scars on one or both faces struck inward from the roughly circular, but occasionally more sub-rectangular or oval, circumference. One face may often be more convex than the other and, in some cases, bears pebble cortex remnants. Sizes range from rare large ones 8–12 centimeters in maximum diameter, through the majority of medium small ones 4–7 centimeters in maximum diameter, down to fairly numerous small ones at 2.5–3.5 centimeters in diameter (pl. 14:1–4).
2. Pebble cores, made on still fully recognizable pebbles, portions, or halves, had flakes nearly always removed on one face in one direction from a single flat striking platform. This may have been nearly circular in the earlier stages of core exploitation but became long and narrow or virtually eliminated as the flaking front approached the cortex-covered rear plane. In cases when this final stage was reached, additional flakes of opportunity were struck from any favorable direction so as to exploit the last bit from the core. In some instances, even the rear cortex surface was invaded or removed. Some of these pebble cores are medium to large in size, retaining much of the original pebble mass, and are 5–8 centimeters in maximum dimension. The great majority, being remnants of core exploitation, are much smaller and range below 5 centimeters down to 2.5 centimeters in diameter. The overall shape is generally a circular pyramid, but elongated ovals and rough rectangular outline forms also occur (pl. 14:5–8).
3. Polyhedral, or amorphous, cores were flaked in several directions on several faces and probably constitute the ultimate, fully exploited stage of the pebble cores and perhaps the discoid cores. One or two specimens are 4.5–5.0 centimeters in maximum diameter, but the bulk is very small, being 2.5–3.0 centimeters in maximum dimension (pl. 14:9–10).

With one or two isolated exceptions in each category made of limestone, all of these cores are made of the various cherts and flints available from among the river cobbles and gravels of the district.

RELATIONSHIP OF THE MONOLITH TO THE OCCUPATION SITE

The visible part of the Barda Balka consolidated spring core monolith stood 3.5 meters high above the ground on the steeply sloping hillside. However, the level of its visible base was close to that of the ancient streamside pebble and gravel beds, which were exposed some 60 meters west on the same hill slope (fig. 2). In other words, this would have placed the active eye of the spring and the active working occupation area of that day at roughly the same level along the streamside terrain of that late Pleistocene time. The monolith consisted of a firmly consolidated limestone conglomerate of small pebbles, gravels, and sands, now virtually masked by close-set lichenous growth. Barely discernable at wide intervals in this cement-hard mass were a few fragments of animal bones and teeth as well as rare artificially struck flint flakes and fragments.

In order to establish the relationship of the monolith and its artifactual contents to the immediately surrounding and underlying deposits, a half-meter-wide trench was dug on either side of the visible base of the monolith. This was 2 meters long and 20–40 centimeters deep on the west and 1.55 meters long and 10–50 centimeters deep on the east (Trenches 9a and 9b, respectively). Removing whatever possible unconsolidated loose sands and gravels that were there exposed most of the circumference of the monolith (here somewhat diminished and disintegrating due to weathering processes at and just below ground level) and revealed that the fine sandy gravelly deposits directly under the monolith were also well cemented and of the same sort and contained traces of flint and bone debris just as up in the consolidated portion of the spring core monolith (table 2 and pl. 15). The two masses merged clearly and seemlessly into each other and were alike in every respect. Blocks of what was evidently the same conglomerate also lay about on the surface near the monolith.

In the course of excavating the conglomerate at and below the visible base of the monolith, it was possible to free a few of the contained flint pieces and bone fragments for study. No example of outstandingly diagnostic types of artifacts was noted, although one or two pieces had edge wear to suggest use as scraping or cutting implements, and there were several small amorphous core fragments (see table 2 and pl. 15). However, it was established that the state of preservation of the flakes, animal bone, and tooth fragments and their general type and appearance matched that of those found in the ancient streamside pebble bed and loose sand and gravel nearby on the west (Trenches 1, 2, 5). The two sets of artifacts are thus considered to be parts of the same archaeological horizon, and both sets of deposits — the ancient streamside sediments, and consolidated sedimentary column and its underpinnings in situ on the hillside — are considered coeval by virtue of sharing the same general artifactual material. Together they record essentially a single occupation period.

Ultimately, it also became clear from the overall conformation of the consolidated sedimentary monolithic column, together with the fully comparable subjacent sediments, that this rock formation was a good example of a dried-up spring core. The entire solidified limestone conglomerate mass represented the channel of an ancient spring-water flow thrusting upward through the hillside beds of sand and gravel. This spring action must have ultimately carried up to at least as far as the present monolith top, and perhaps somewhat farther, to reach the ground surface of its day. Subsequently, the major post-glacial erosion cycle cut back down through the massive Jarmo silts. It also carved out the local dry-stream gully to its present-day state and gradually laid bare the upper meters of the dry spring core, which was solidified in place to become the present-day monolithic standing stone. Evidently, too, the spring may have served as a focus for some part of the widely scattered occupation site, to judge by the artifactual debris and faunal remains contained in the consolidated spring-core sediments since, as noted, they match up well with the artifactual debris and the scanty faunal material from the pebble bed and the gravel and sand pit to the west (table 2).

Table 2. Flint artifacts extracted from the limestone conglomerate spring deposit*

	From in Situ in Above-ground Deposit of Monolith	*From Blocks of Limestone Conglomerate Scattered near Monolith*
Pieces with Edge Flaking: Scrapers or Notched Flakes	1	1
Core Fragments	1	2
Trimming Debris without Edge Flaking	9	11
Total	**11**	**14**

* This material is not included in the definitive tallies and analyses dealing with the main part of this site and report.

FAUNAL REMAINS

Virtually all of the limited body of poorly preserved and fragmentary animal bones and teeth excavated at Barda Balka was found intermingled with the stone industry in the jumbled, largely unsorted stream gravel deposit exposed in Trench 5. This was situated 1 meter east of the exposed part of the stream pebble bed sector of the occupation site (fig. 2).

The few identifiable pieces culled from this friable material comprised bones, teeth, and tooth fragments. After an informal immediate survey in the field in 1951 by Fredrik Barth, then of the Ethnographic Museum of the University of Oslo, these were ultimately studied by Dr. F. C. Fraser of the British Museum of Natural History, to which the material was permanently consigned. Fraser reported (letter of July 1952 to R. J. Braidwood) the presence of the following species: elephant, rhinoceros, ox, sheep or goat, and an equid that was possibly onager, and also of the land snail *Helix salomonica* identified by Mr. Wilkins of the same museum. This information may be expanded a little by some of the field observations of Barth, who noted that the equid bones were present in some quantity and that there were also fragments of turtle carapace present (Wright and Howe 1951, p. 109). Still further observations by Reed (Braidwood and Howe 1960, pp. 164–65) were that the ox was about the size of *Bos primigenius*, the elephant the Indian elephant, and the equid suggestive of onager but not actually identifiable as such, and that the mammal species reported were not helpful climatic indicators since they were all widely distributed over a long range of time. Reed did, however, at the same time note that the presence of *Helix salomonica*, a form common nowadays in much of this foothill area, indicated a climate resembling that of today.

DISCOVERY OF ANCIENT BLOOD RESIDUES ON ARTIFACTS

In 1984, microscopic organic traces of ancient blood were found on the surface of selected test artifacts from Barda Balka (pl. 16:1). This evidence was established by Thomas H. Loy, then of the British Columbia Provincial Museum. He had recently developed methods for the detection and identification of ancient blood residues of humans and of a few mammal forms (Loy 1983, 1985). (On the evolution of scholarship about ancient blood, see Yorke Rowan's *Foreword*. — Ed.)

During the following year, tests were performed on these residues. The initial test was the extraction and crystallization of the hemoglobin present in the blood residues. Additional immunological tests further verified the presence of both human and animal blood deposits on the artifacts (personal communication, May 1987, Andrée R. Wood, research assistant, Oriental Institute Joint Prehistoric Project).

Lately, more detailed observations on two artifacts were reported. More particularly, these confirmed the presence on one biface of a residue of human blood on one edge and of wood, probably conifer, on the opposite edge (Loy 1992).

For the present, the theoretical dating of this archaeological material should reasonably be confined to the time bracket of 60,000–100,000/120,000 years B.P. (on dates, see *Foreword*). This was assigned to the specifically related deposits at the site, as a result of the local geomorphological studies and general geological reasoning of Herbert E. Wright, who studied both the site itself and a wide region around it (see above). Furthermore, speculation as to the human types that might be possibly associated with the site and its industry must perforce remain in the suspense file for lack of evidence, direct or indirect.

EVIDENCE FOR A BUTCHERING SITE

The occurrence, type, and physical condition of animal bones and teeth found in association with the stone assemblage at this single early occupation horizon are the principal grounds for considering that the site of Barda Balka was, in part, a wild animal-butchering site. Emplaced upon the pebbles, gravels, and sands of a dry stream bed close to a spring, numerous long bones and others as well as a few teeth were found whole or broken into relatively small pieces. Virtually all this material, comprising some few whole bones, the identifiable teeth, and tooth fragments, was found in the unsorted gravels and sands of Trench 5. It occurred jumbled at all levels therein for the one-meter depth that the excavation penetrated there. Such traces were probably fortuitously so concentrated at that spot probably by stream action and were not at all in evidence in the exposed part of the closely adjacent, somewhat higher-lying pebble bed. It is possible that most of the bone was indeed originally entirely concentrated nearby in one or more localized butchering sites on the sand and gravel deposit and that the stoneworking area lay well apart in an area of coarser pebbles and cobbles somewhat withdrawn from, above and away from, the spring and its immediate surroundings.

The bone fragments were angular and friable, well weathered, some showing the tiny vermicular surface grooves due to decomposition from close-pressing plant rootlets. As a result of the considerable attrition and defacement due to the extensive fragmentation and the natural decomposition on the bone surfaces, there were no observed signs of hacking, striations, pecking, pounding, or other marks of possible butchering. These specimens appeared too weathered and their surfaces too eroded and defaced to retain such secondary traces of human work. Thus, no convincing evidence for deliberate purposeful breakage or cutting was noticed. The evidence for a deliberate purposeful butchering site is simply the marked and otherwise unlikely concentration here of bones and teeth of a variety of large-sized game animals in one place, that is, *Elephas*, rhinoceros, *Bos*, *Ovis*, *Capra*, and an equid.

RECENT MATERIALS FROM SURFACE AND DERIVED DEPOSIT

Aside from the materials found in situ in the pebble bed, the gravel bed, and the spring core limestone conglomerate, there were very limited quantities of archaeological materials found on the surface and in the slopewash at the various trenches or elsewhere. The derived slopewash deposit lay in very thin layers of green or reddish buff silts overlying the occupation horizon and the various natural layers.

POTTERY AND OTHER RECENT MATERIALS

The scarce pottery and still scarcer glass and iron found at Barda Balka came from either the surface and/or slopewash in the topmost centimeters of the trenches dug. The greatest part of the pottery was undistinquished recent-looking brick-red hard wheelmade wares. A few other fragments each of handmade plain ware, wheelmade gray-green, blue glaze or green glaze and stone wares completed the list. There were also a very few clear glass bits and one iron nail. All these elements may unquestionably be viewed as recent and be dismissed from further consideration. They were the only modern materials found. Indeed, they are testimony to the uncluttered character of this prehistoric site.

STONE MATERIAL

No identifiable lithic material of other periods than that of the single occupation horizon reported were found.

ARTIFACTS FROM BARDA BALKA DEPOSITED IN MUSEUMS

In May 1951, a representative cross section of artifactual materials from the soundings at Barda Balka was deposited permanently at the Directorate General of Antiquities in Baghdad and became part of the collections at the National Museum there. Although the selection was made on the basis of a preliminary typological classification of all the material originally drawn up after sorting in the field, it nevertheless conformed closely to the scheme of the final typological categories adopted in this report. It must be noted that the quantities of pebble tools and core bifaces (as opposed to various scrapers and other flake artifacts) in that early selected cross section were deliberately kept low. This was due to the fact that an ample sampling of these two categories was already in the national holdings from previous official and other authorized collections made at the site. It was considered advisable to keep together as many specimens as possible of these newly excavated key categories for definitive study and final description in this report.

The specimens deposited in Baghdad have, with two exceptions, not been included in the tallies used in this major study. These exceptions are the unique trihedral pick (illustrated in Wright and Howe 1951), and one of the two specimens of polyhedral flaked spheres, or "boules." In these particular instances, both these significant types are included in the final tallies of this report and are also listed in the series left in Baghdad.

Furthermore, a small untallied selection (less than a dozen pieces) was also deposited at the laboratory of the prehistoric section of the Musée de l'Homme in Paris. In addition, the Peabody Museum of Harvard University has a small collection of surface material from Barda Balka, presented by Henry Field.

The 119 artifacts from the Barda Balka soundings of May 1951 deposited in Baghdad are as follows in table 3:

Table 3. Artifacts deposited at the National Museum of Iraq

Category	Type	Number
Pebble Tools	Choppers	8
	Chopping Tools	2
	Bipolar Pebble Tool	1
	Polyhedral Sphere, or "Boule"	1
	Total	12
Core Bifaces	Cordiform	1
	Pebble Butted	1
	Trihedral Pick	1
	Total	3
Flake Artifacts	Large Flake Scrapers	2
	Side Scrapers	7
	Discoid Scrapers	7
	Concave, Hollow Scrapers and Notched Flakes, Fragments	37
	Steep Scraper	1
	Flakes, Fragments with Steep Alternate Face Edgewear/Flaking	4
	Used Flakes, Fragments	34
	Trimming Flakes, Fragments	4
	Total	96
Cores	Discoid	4
	Pebble	2
	Polyhedral, Amorphous	2
	Total	8
	Combined Total	**119**

COMPARISONS

There are as yet virtually no other specific sites with assemblages that clearly match the general morphology of that at Barda Balka. There are, however, several individual implement types associated with Middle Paleolithic horizons found at Barda Balka that occur in various combinations elsewhere, reviewed below. The main typological elements that go to make up the industry found at Barda Balka may be summarized as follows:

Type	*Number*	*Percentage*
Pebble Tools	197	17
Core Bifaces	57	5
Flake Implements	898	78
Total	**1,152**	**100**

The details of these three general categories are given here:

1. Pebble tools, comprising choppers, chopping tools, and a very few related sub-types such as bipolar and the pointed, more fully flaked, forms approaching the core biface in outline are all made on limestone stream pebbles. All are shaped by the removal of a few broad invasive flakes, and nearly all have additional edge flaking or low-grade flaking of steep, squamous, or step scars evidently from use alone and only rarely any neater flaking suggesting retouch.

   The very rare polyhedral spheroids, or "boules" here are also a typical component of the pebble tool tradition. This has a long history in Lower Paleolithic and Middle Paleolithic times.
2. Core bifaces are predominantly of flint, although a very few of limestone are also found. In the aggregate, their several outline shapes are clearly akin to a number of those found in the Upper Acheulean tradition: the silhouette outlines include heart-shaped, pear-shaped, and almond-shaped forms and a broad-ended cleaver, or "hachereau" form. A single coarse trihedral pick was also part of the tool kit here. Very rarely, there are tapering elongated forms that approach the Micoquean type (often considered a guide fossil indicator of late or final Acheulean), but at Barda Balka they lack its exaggeratedly attenuated point and its bulging thick butt end, and so cannot strictly be considered Micoquean. The edges of the core bifaces here range from fine and straight to somewhat coarse and more sinuous. The related flaked surfaces combine both the broad shallow wood-on-stone and the more deeply cut stone-on-stone sort of flake scar.
3. Flake implements and miscellaneous flake pieces and fragments (exclusive of used pieces and trimming debris) are numerous and irregular, crudely struck and coarse. In many cases they display edge flaking. In some cases this may be rather neat and regular and well developed and controlled looking; but the great majority of cases display considerable edge wear of miscellaneous sorts (including some natural attrition) discontinuously along their periphery. Such coarse irregular crude flake and fragment pieces occur in many Lower and Middle Paleolithic contexts alongside pebble and core biface artifacts and are notable in Tayacian-type flake assemblages of the Middle Paleolithic.

The conjunction of pebble tools, core bifaces, and coarse irregular flake implements has been reported from a number of Lower and Middle Paleolithic sites in East and South Asia, across the Indian Peninsula to the Horn of Africa, East and South Africa, as well as in North Africa and Western and Central Europe. Selected sites of interest are summarized below.

Sidi Zin, Tunisia

Sidi Zin in central Tunisia is an open-air occupation site with big-game mammalian remains and a stone industry made on materials drawn from nearby sources. The occupation site was found in massive semi-consolidated gravels close by a spring. The site was found by E.-G. Gobert, the lithic materials assessed by him (Gobert 1950), and the fauna studied by R. Vaufrey (Vaufrey 1950).

The stone industry at Sidi Zin generally resembles that at Barda Balka. It contained plentiful limestone pebble tools and numerous irregular flake artifacts and core bifaces of quartzite and flint and some limestone. The distinctive elongated "Micoquean" biface form suggested a late Upper Acheulean cultural stage. The big-game mammalian fauna was broadly Upper Pleistocene in character. It consisted of a basic North African group of rhinoceros, equus, antelope, gazelle, and giant ox, with elephant only in the lowest level, and with the subsequent addition of gnu and, in the upper level, sheep. The overall character suggests later rather than earlier time.

Although the site remains geologically unanchored, the fauna suggests a Late Pleistocene time frame and the stone industry a Late Middle Paleolithic cultural stage. This inconclusive evidence places Sidi Zin somewhat later than Barda Balka on slim typological and faunal grounds but implies a similar hunting-gathering level of existence.

Ubeidiya, Israel

Ubeidiya is a sizeable and complex area of ancient encampments containing an assemblage of pebble tool, core biface, and flake artifacts that are found within massive consolidated stream gravels and varying estuarine lake deposits in the central Jordan River Valley just south of Lake Kinneret (Sea of Galilee) in Israel. Known since 1959, it was meticulously excavated by numerous investigators during the period of 1962–1974; and its geology, various fauna, and lithic assemblages have been well documented and interpreted (Bar-Yosef and Goren-Inbar 1993).

The sequence of gravel and silt deposits containing the occupation horizons lies as a contiguous series of near-vertical truncated conglomerate blocks exposed by the erosion of overlying surface silt beds on the west side of the Jordan River. Violent earthquakes that evidently produced these up-ended deposits are a feature of conditions prevailing within the supra-continental Rift Zone that extends from East Africa into the Near East. The Jordan Valley is a major northern segment of this seismic zone and is thus subject to periodic quakes.

The site appears to be a series of occupation floors in stream-bank and lake-edge positions with fluctuating shore patterns and shifting encampments. Two particular related localities, LT 15 and LT 26, out of the dozens of excavated loci, provided the most plentiful samples of the lithic industry and were chosen to best document it. The raw materials used came from nearby natural sources containing a variety of rock types, but flint was the predominant material.

Distinct types of artifacts included fairly plentiful pebble choppers and chopping tools; rarer bifacial core tools such as picks, cleavers, and double-pointed, pear-shaped, and other handaxes; a number of trihedrals and spheroids; quantities of irregular flakes variously re-touched or used as side scrapers; end scrapers; notched, denticulated, or nosed pieces; awls; and rare possible burins. Finally, a few discoid and amorphous cores and plentiful undistinctive trimming debris complete the assemblage. Although it shares with Barda Balka a number of individual types as well as the reduced quantity of core biface artifacts and the spectrum of different crude irregular flake implements, the coarser character of the bifaces, the relative quantities, and overall morphology of the assemblage are not especially close to those of Barda Balka. The two sites simply share a similar level of hunting-gathering existence.

In addition, the fauna is largely of lacustrine and fluvial molluscs and fish with a considerable further mammal component. This mammal fauna was identified as partly Villafranchian, or early Pleistocene, and partly also as mid-Pleistocene. The various aquatic fauna likewise had a relatively early cast. Thus Ubeidiya represents a long lower to middle Pleistocene span and predates Barda Balka by a considerable margin.

Sites in the Ladiz and Mashkid River Valleys, Iran

The Ladiz and Mashkid River Valleys in the Sarhadd Plateau in southeastern Iran have a number of widely separated surface and stream terrace sites that contain examples of the well-known and widespread pebble chopper/chopping-tool complex of industries. Gary W. Hume discovered these Iranian sites during a survey in the 1970s and named the industry "Ladizian" as another regional isolate within the overarching chopper/chopping-tool cultural horizon (Hume 1976). Of several localities, two, LT2 and LT8, furnished most of the materials.

The first locality, LT2, was a surface scatter several hundred thousand square meters in extent up on the plateau flanking the Ladiz River Valley. It lay near the edge of the topmost river gravels (T1), 60 meters above the present-day river alluvium, with five descending fluvial terraces extending in between. The scatter was considered an essentially intact occupation floor of virtually fresh artifacts in situ. Based on a surface collection of some 300 artifacts comprising various pebble tools and irregular flake artifacts, primarily of quarztite, this combination of lithic types only broadly resembles that at Barda Balka, lacking core bifaces. No faunal remains were found; and it was not possible to place the site in a confirmed geological context.

The second locality, LT8, consisted of a presumably derived formation, containing artifacts, which lay in an erosional depression cut into the T1 surface near the top of the local last erosional cycle. About two hundred artifacts were collected, and these reflected the same typology as those at LT2. It, too, lacked fauna and could not be geologically dated. Both sites lay at the top and early end of the last major local erosion cycle and are comparatively integral concentrations of artifacts, the one suggesting an authentic occupation site, the other derived traces of another. From their typological aspect, they appear to be of a Middle Paleolithic cultural stage; and from their physical circumstances and position on the terrain, they might possibly be considered as mid-Pleistocene in age. However, their age cannot be surely determined.

This southeastern Iranian trace of the pebble chopper/chopping-tool complex simply serves to indicate that this level of hunting-gathering existence prevailed at some undetermined early time in this quarter. Well west of the long-known classic province on the Indian Peninsula and in Southeast Asia, it fills in another point on the distribution map somewhat closer geographically to the occurrence at Barda Balka.

CONCLUSIONS

A particular assemblage of pebble, core biface, and flake artifacts, discovered in 1949, was investigated further by the four-day soundings of 1951. These showed stream-bed gravels and a conglomerate fossil spring core that contained scanty fragmentary remains of big-game animals, and the debris of stone-working activities. There were large components of pebble and irregular flake artifacts, and a very limited component of a variety of distinctive well-made, straight-edged bifacial core artifacts to indicate an Upper Acheulean cultural stage of the Middle Paleolithic. The very limited and fragmentary remains of big-game animals were those of banal species and indicated climatic and ecological regimes that were essentially no different from those of the present-day in the area. However, their presence hints at butchering activity. The whole suggests an occupation site marked by an extended, or else repeated short-term, kind of encampment by hunter-gatherers with stone-working and animal-butchering activities being carried out near a streamside spring.

However, geomorphological and geological studies have rather clearly fixed the site tentatively to the stage of transition between the end of the last interglacial and the begining of the last glacial; and this stage may at present be placed theoretically in the time span of 60,000–120,000 years B.P. (On dates, see *Foreword*.)

Barda Balka thus joins the ranks of the widespread complex of chopper/chopping-tool industries now known to extend from East and Southeast Asia across the Indian Peninsula, through the Near East, to Africa and Europe. While many of these sites remain unfixed in geological time, some have shown by their geological and faunal contexts that they belong to the early and middle Pleistocene time range and to Lower and Early Middle Paleolithic cultural stages. None, however, can be clearly matched by their stoneworking, faunal, or geological aspects to the Barda Balka materials. Thus, Barda Balka, with its relatively late geological context, appears as a late-surviving example of this long-lasting and widespread stage of human culture of the hunting-gathering stage.

CONCORDANCE

OIM No.	*Description*	*Provenience*	*Illustration Reference*
A64858	Biface, traces of blood analyzed by Tom Loy	Unknown	pl. 16:1
A66500	Biface	Unknown	pl. 16:2
A66501	Biface	Trench 2	pl. 16:3
A66502	Biface	Trench 3	pl. 16:4
A66503	Biface	Trench 4	pl. 16:5
A66504	Cleaver, "hachereau"	Surface	pl. 11:2
A66505	Biface	Unknown	pl. 16:6
A66506	Pebble chopper	Unknown	pl. 16:7
A66550	Micoque-like biface	Pebble bed, in situ	pl. 11:1
A66551	Biface	Surface	pl. 10:2
A66553	Hollow scraper	In decomposing conglomerate around base of the monolith, in situ	pl. 15:5
A66554	Flake tool: converging side scraper	Gravel bed, in situ	pl. 12:9
A66555	Flake tool: elongated, rectilinear side scraper	Gravel bed, in situ	pl. 12:2
A66556	Flake tool: scraper with alternate opposite-edge flaking	Pebble bed, in situ	pl. 13:15
A166082	Truncated pebble	Pebble bed, in situ	pl. 7:1
A166083	Truncated pebble	Pebble bed, in situ	pl. 7:2
A166084	Pebble scraper	Pebble bed, in situ	pl. 7:3
A166085	Pebble chopper	Gravel bed, in situ	pl. 7:4
A166086	Pebble chopper	Gravel bed, in situ	pl. 7:5
A166087	Pebble chopper	Gravel bed, in situ	pl. 7:6
A166088	Pebble chopper on flake	Pebble bed, in situ	pl. 7:7
A166089	Pebble chopper	Gravel bed, in situ	pl. 8:1
A166090	Pebble chopper	Gravel bed, in situ	pl. 8:2
A166091	Bipolar pebble tool	Gravel bed, in situ	pl. 8:3
A166092	Bipolar pebble tool	Pebble bed, in situ	pl. 8:4
A166093	Bipolar pebble tool	Pebble bed, in situ	pl. 8:5
A166094	Polyhedral spheroid	Surface	pl. 9:1
A166095	Biface	Pebble bed, in situ	pl. 9:2
A166096	Biface	Pebble bed, in situ	pl. 9:3
A166097	Biface	Pebble bed, in situ	pl. 10:1
A166098	Biface	Pebble bed, in situ	pl. 10:3
A166099	Flake tool: elongated, rectilinear side scraper	Gravel bed, in situ	pl. 12:1
A166100	Flake tool: elongated, rectilinear side scraper	Gravel bed, in situ	pl. 12:3
A166101	Flake tool: elongated, rectilinear side scraper	Gravel bed, in situ	pl. 12:4
A166102	Flake tool: elongated, rectilinear side scraper	Gravel bed, in situ	pl. 12:5
A166103	Flake tool: converging side scraper	Pebble bed, in situ	pl. 12:6
A166104	Flake tool: converging side scraper	Gravel bed, in situ	pl. 12:7
A166105	Flake tool: converging side scraper	Gravel bed, in situ	pl. 12:8

OIM No.	Description	Provenience	Illustration Reference
A166106	Flake tool: side scraper	Gravel bed, in situ	pl. 12:10
A166107	Flake tool: side scraper	Gravel bed, in situ	pl. 12:11
A166108	Flake tool: side scraper	Gravel bed, in situ	pl. 12:12
A166109	Flake tool: side scraper	Gravel bed, in situ	pl. 12:13
A166110	Flake tool: side scraper	Gravel bed, in situ	pl. 12:14
A166111	Flake tool: side scraper	Gravel bed, in situ	pl. 12:15
A166112	Flake tool: side scraper	Gravel bed, in situ	pl. 12:16
A166113	Flake tool: side scraper	Pebble bed, in situ	pl. 12:17
A166114	Flake tool: rounded scraper	Pebble bed, in situ	pl. 13:1
A166115	Flake tool: rounded scraper	Gravel bed, in situ	pl. 13:2
A166116	Flake tool: rounded scraper	Gravel bed, in situ	pl. 13:3
A166117	Flake tool: rounded scraper	Gravel bed, in situ	pl. 13:4
A166118	Flake tool: rounded scraper	Gravel bed, in situ	pl. 13:5
A166119	Flake tool: concave scraper	Gravel bed, in situ	pl. 13:6
A166120	Flake tool: concave scraper	Gravel bed, in situ	pl. 13:7
A166121	Flake tool: concave scraper	Gravel bed, in situ	pl. 13:8
A166122	Flake tool: concave scraper	Gravel bed, in situ	pl. 13:9
A166123	Flake tool: notched scraping tool	Gravel bed, in situ	pl. 13:10
A166124	Flake tool: notched scraping tool	Gravel bed, in situ	pl. 13:11
A166125	Flake tool: notched scraping tool	Gravel bed, in situ	pl. 13:12
A166126	Flake tool: steep scraper	Pebble bed, in situ	pl. 13:13
A166127	Flake tool: end scraper	Gravel bed, in situ	pl. 13:14
A166128	Flake tool: scraper with alternate opposite-edge flaking	Unknown	pl. 13:16
A166129	Discoid core	Pebble bed, in situ	pl. 14:1
A166130	Discoid core	Pebble bed, in situ	pl. 14:2
A166131	Discoid core	Gravel bed, in situ	pl. 14:3
A166132	Discoid core	Pebble bed, in situ	pl. 14:4
A166133	Pebble core	Gravel bed, in situ	pl. 14:5
A166134	Pebble core	Gravel bed, in situ	pl. 14:6
A166135	Pebble core	Gravel bed, in situ	pl. 14:7
A166136	Pebble core	Gravel bed, in situ	pl. 14:8
A166137	Polyhedral, amorphous core	Gravel bed, in situ	pl. 14:9
A166138	Polyhedral, amorphous core	Gravel bed, in situ	pl. 14:10
A166139	Pebble core fragment	Subterranean part of the monolith, in situ	pl. 15:1
A166140	Pebble core fragment	Subterranean part of the monolith, in situ	pl. 15:2
A166141	Polyhedral core	Subterranean part of the monolith, in situ	pl. 15:3
A166142	Notched flake	Subterranean part of the monolith, in situ	pl. 15:4
A166143	Notched flake	In decomposing conglomerate around base of the monolith, in situ	pl. 15:6
A166144	Notched flake	In decomposing conglomerate around base of the monolith, in situ	pl. 15:7

PLATES

a

b

Barda Balka. (*a*) Center (from left to right): Bruce Howe, Robert J. Braidwood, Charles A. Reed(?), and Linda S. Braidwood. (*b*) Center (from left to right) Robert J. Braidwood, Bruce Howe, Charles A. Reed(?), Linda S. Braidwood, and Herbert E. Wright Jr.(?). Photos by Gustavus Swift Jr. Presumed to be taken during excavation, in May 1951

a

b

Barda Balka. (*a*) (from left to right) Bruce Howe, Linda S. Braidwood, and Robert J. Braidwood. (*b*) Overview of the area immediately surrounding Barda Balka, which can be seen at the top of the hill in the center of the photograph. Photos by Gustavus Swift Jr. Presumed to be taken during excavation, in May 1951

Plate 3

Monolith from west, standing 3.5 m high; showing state of the consolidated gravel conglomerate column in spring 1951. Earth at below-ground level removed to show natural continuity of monolith with underlying consolidated sedimentary deposits

West face of monolith below ground in Trench 9a, showing unity of formation above and below ground. Meter stick on right lies at ground level

Plate 5

Close-up of west face of monolith below ground level showing artiodactyl tooth fragment, lower left, and numerous flint trimming flakes and fragments all in situ in matrix of conglomerate column of monolith

Pebble bed, Trench 3, looking north, 60 m west of monolith, showing flint biface, left center, among stream pebbles. Overlying silts and slope wash extending up to ground surface in background at top of photograph

Pebble tools, photos and drawings: (*1–2*) truncated pebbles (A166082–83); (*3*) pebble scraper (A166084); (*4–6*) pebble choppers (A166085–87); (*7*) pebble chopper on flake (A166088)

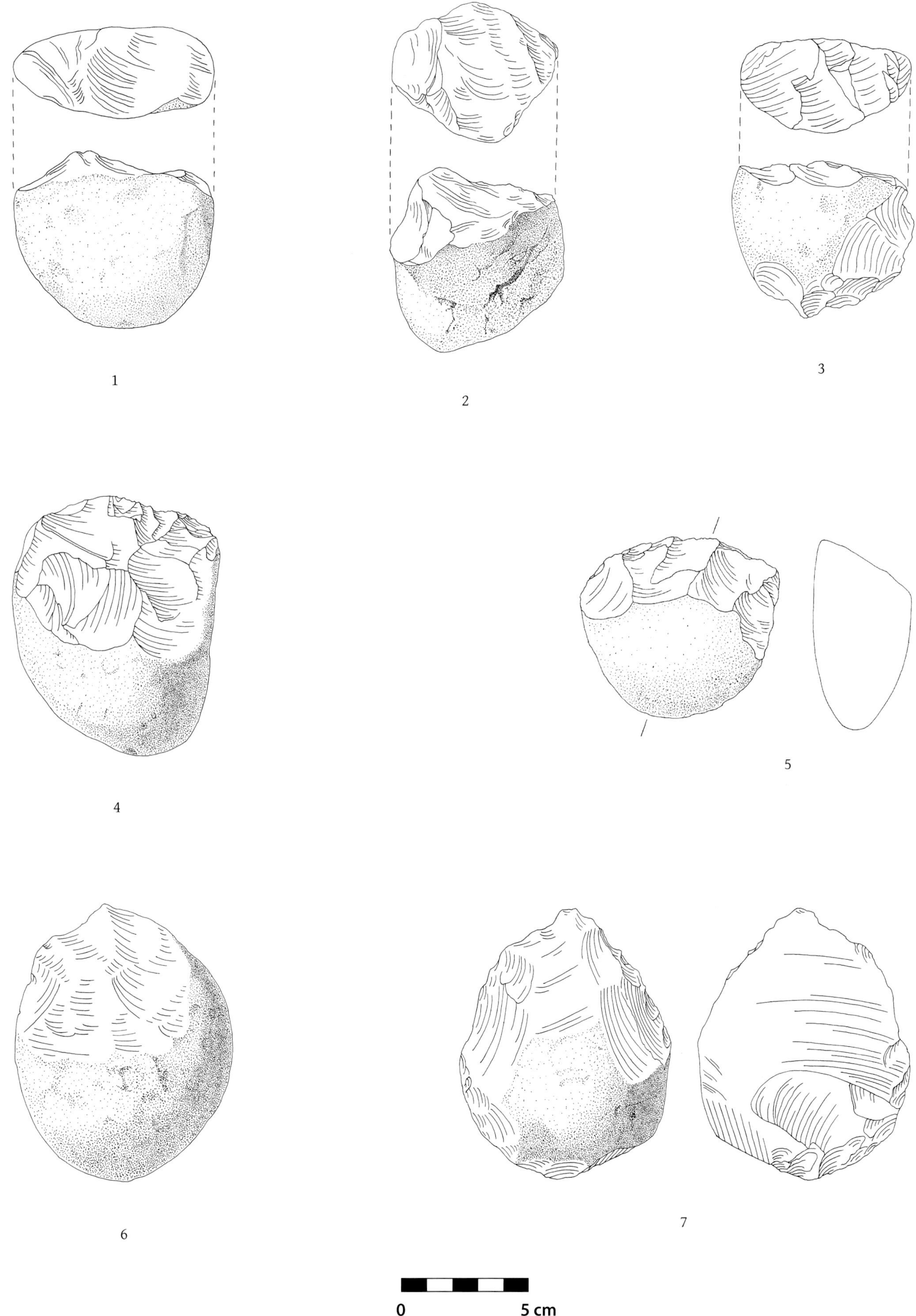
1
2
3
4
5
6
7
0
5 cm

Pebble tools, photos and drawings: (*1–2*) pebble chopping tools (A166089, A166090); (*3–5*) bipolar pebble tools (A166091, A166092, A166093)

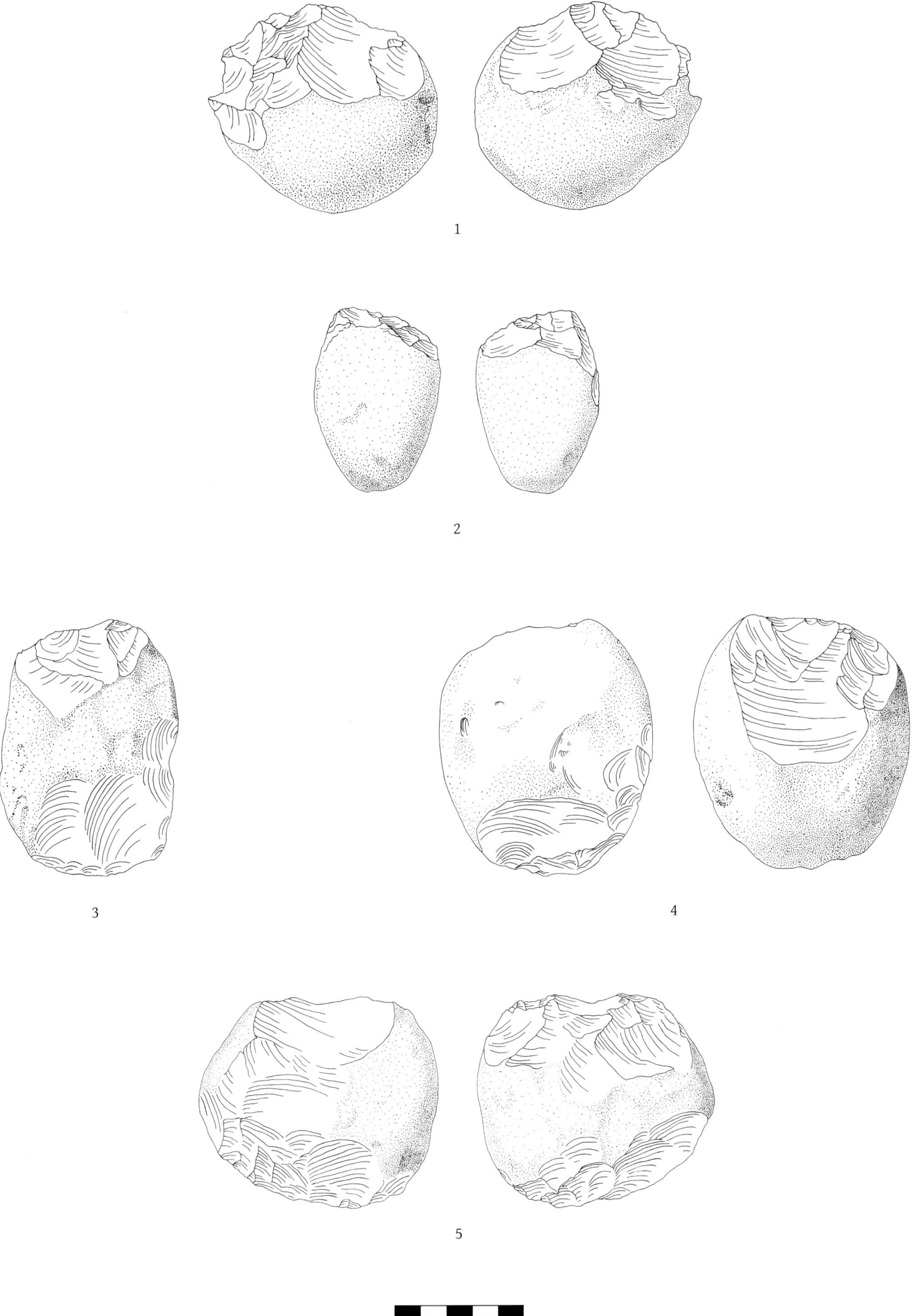
1
2
3
4
5
0
5 cm

Plate 9a

Polyhedral spheroid and bifaces, photos and drawings: (*1*) polyhedral spheroid (A166094); (*2-3*) bifaces (A166095, A166096)

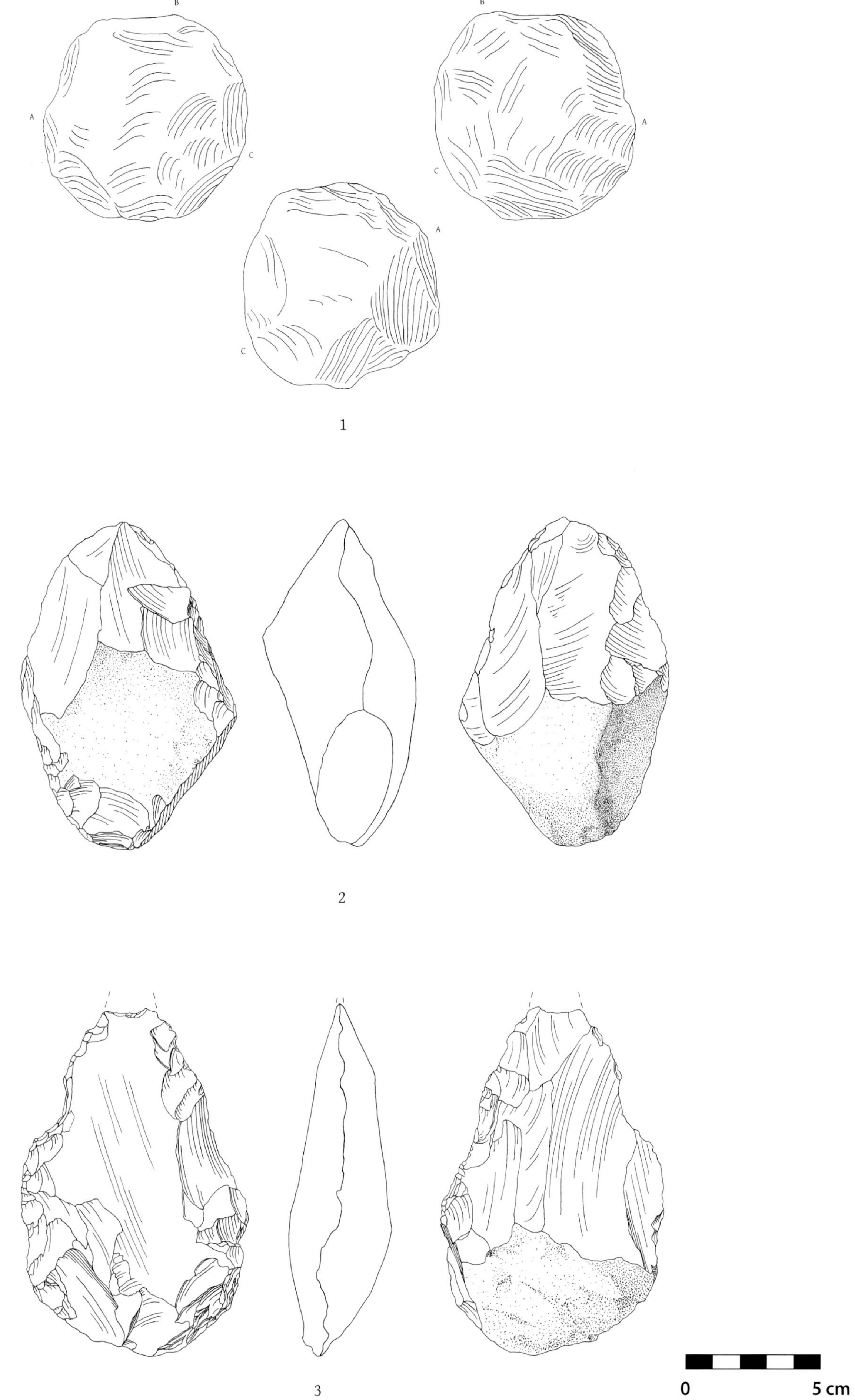
B
A
C
B
A
C
A
C
1
2
3
0
5 cm

Bifaces, photos and drawings: (*1*) A166097, (*2*) A66551, (*3*) A166098

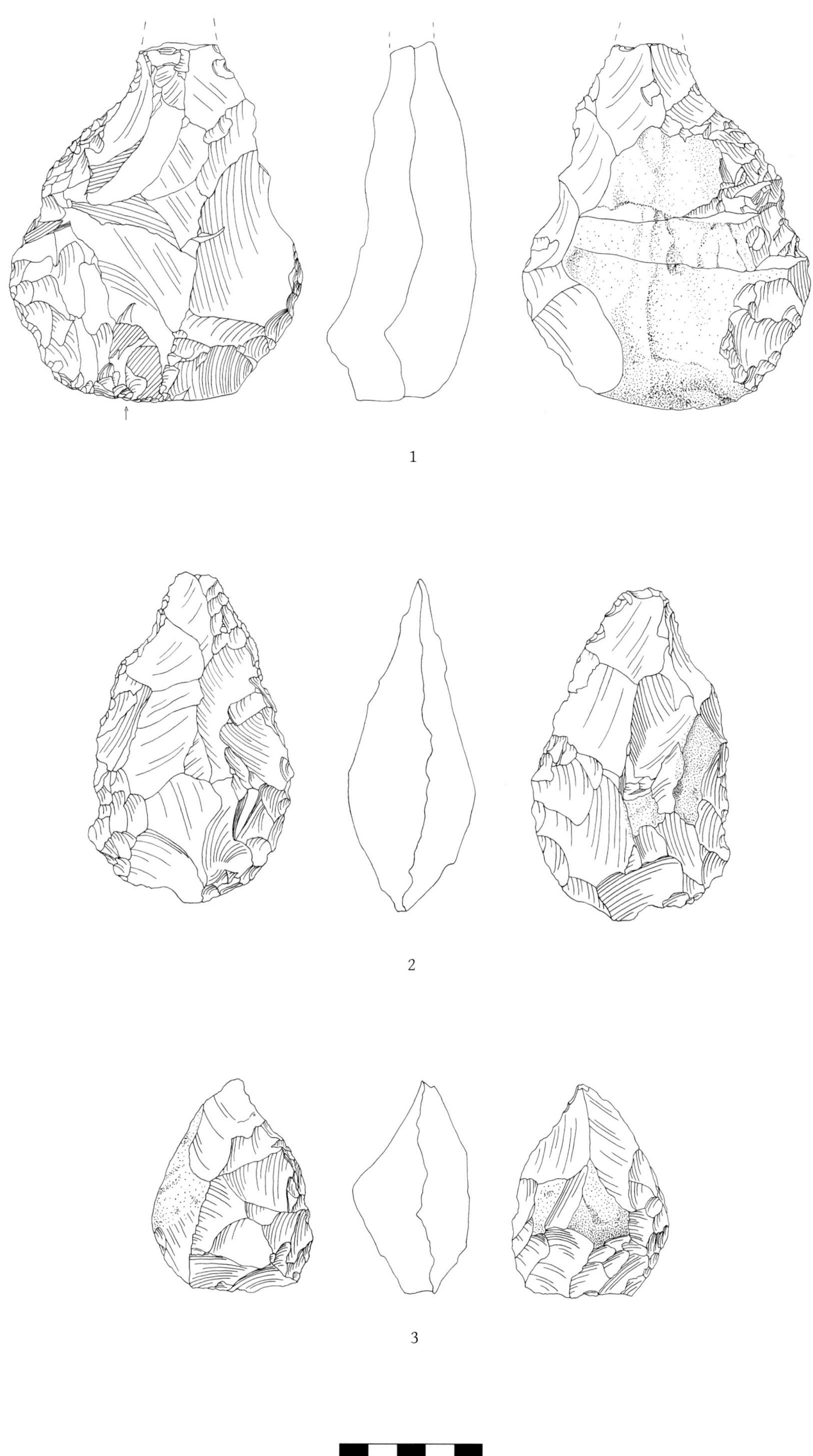
1
2
3
0
5 cm

1

2

Bifaces, photos and drawings: (*1*) Micoque-like biface (A66550); (*2*) cleaver, “hachereau” (A66504)

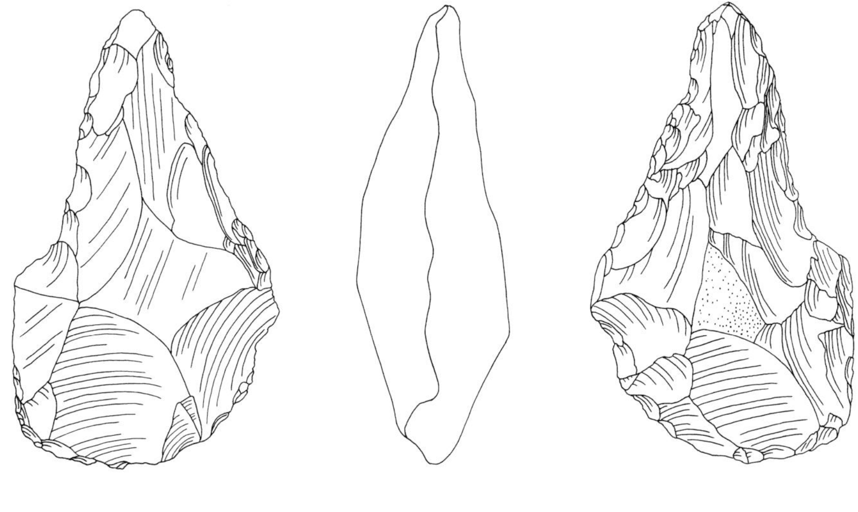

1

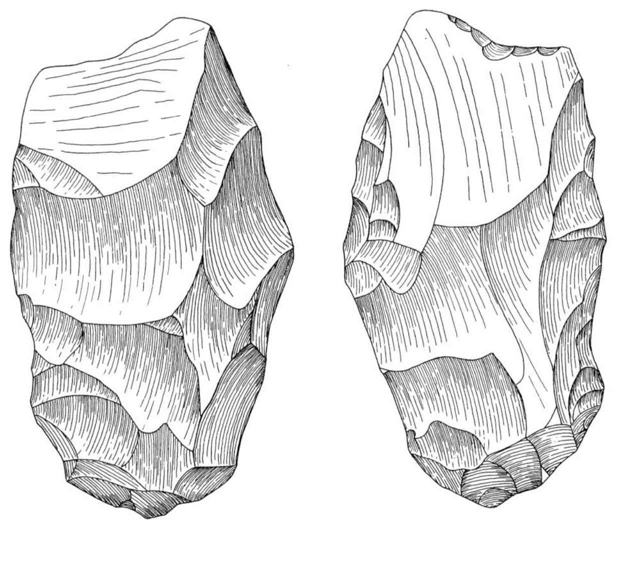

2

0 5 cm

Flake tools, photos and drawings. Side scrapers: (*1–5*) elongated, rectilinear (A166099, A66555, A166100, A166101, A166102); (*6–9*) converging (A166103, A166104, A166105, A66554); (*10–17*) various on irregular flakes, fragments (A166106, A166107, A166108, A166109, A166110, A166111, A166112, A166113)

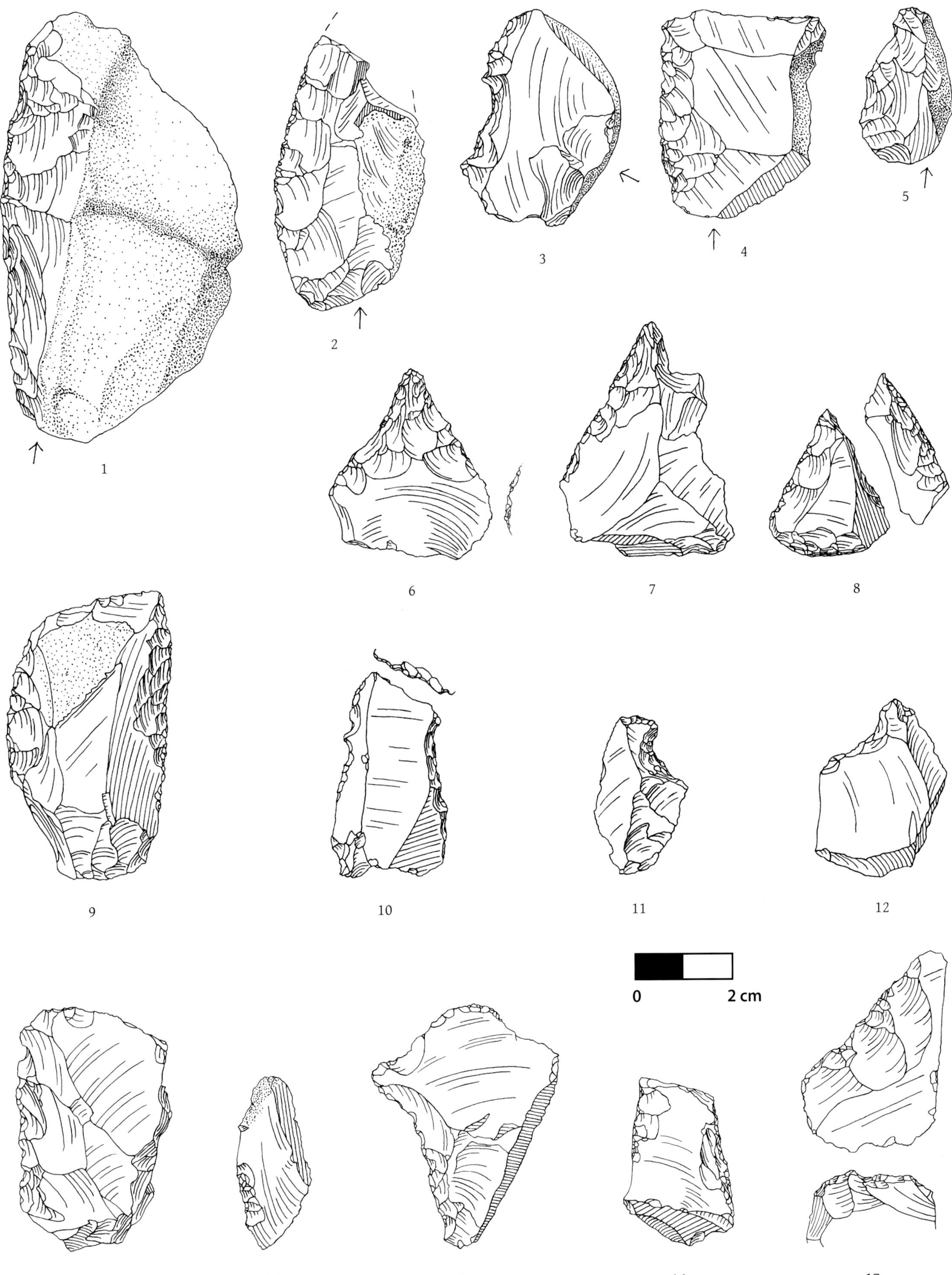
1
2
3
4
5
6
7
8
9
10
11
12
13
14
15
16
17
0
2 cm

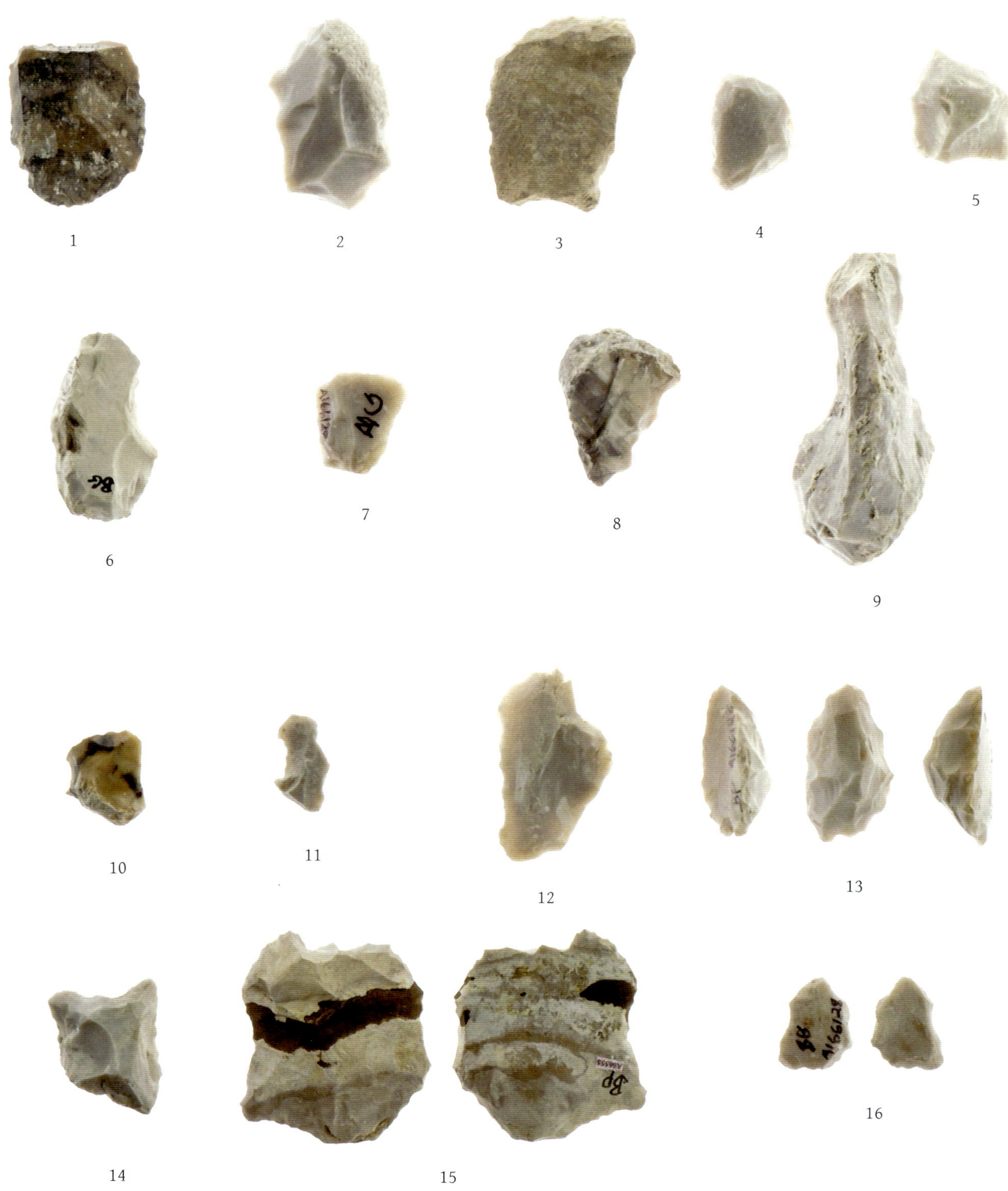

Flake tools, photos and drawings. Various scraping tools: (*1–5*) rounded scrapers (A166114, A166115, A166116, A166117, A166118); (*6–9*) concave scrapers (A166119, A166120, A166121, A166122); (*10–12*) notched pieces (A166123, A166124, A166125); (*13*) steep scraper (A166126); (*14*) end scraper (A166127); (*15–16*) pieces with alternate opposite-edge flaking (A66556, A166128)

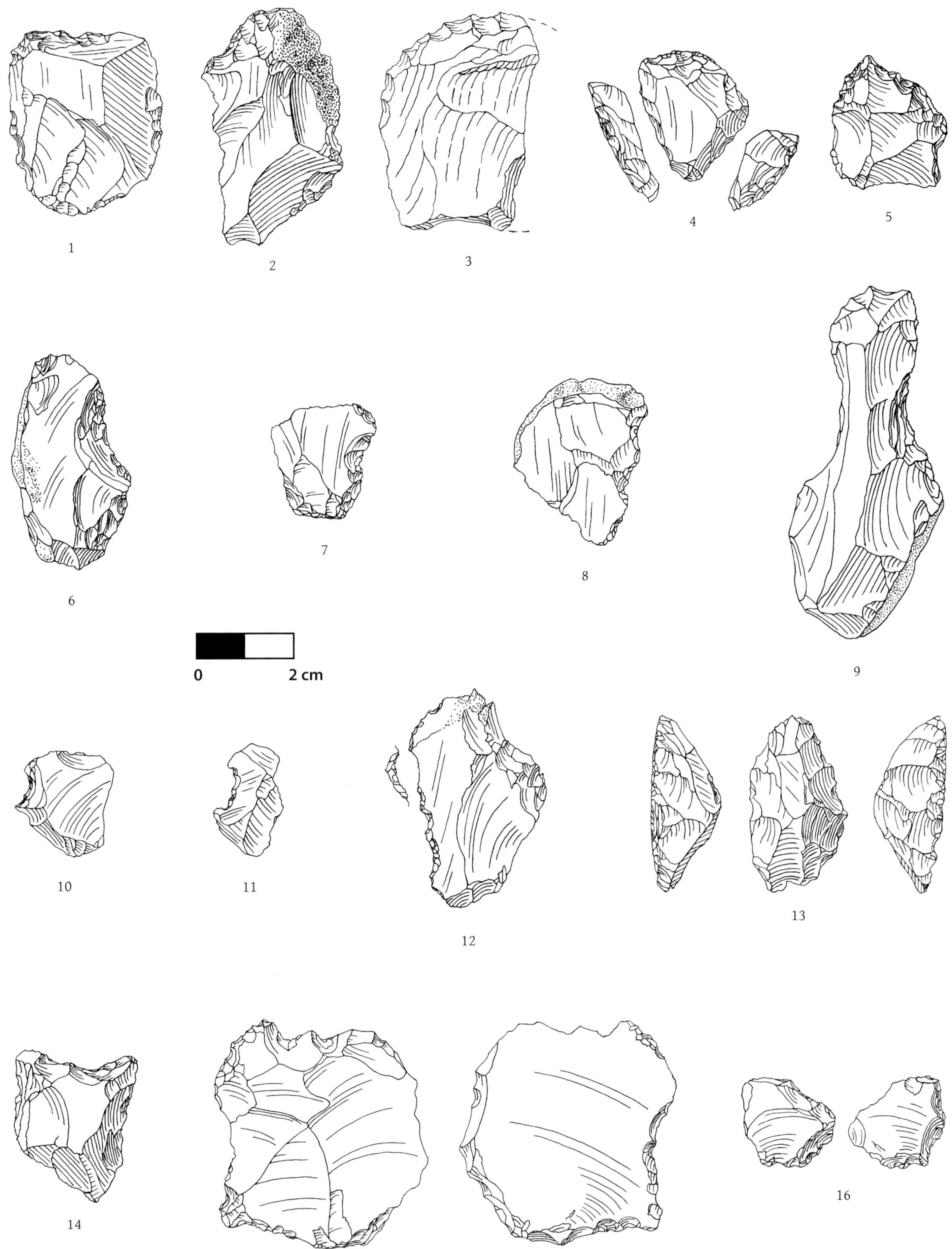
1
2
3
4
5
6
7
8
9
0
2 cm
10
11
12
13
14
15
16

Cores, photos and drawings. (*1–4*) Discoid (A166129, A166130, A166131, A166132); (*5–8*) pebble (A166133, A166134, A166135, A166136); (*9–10*) polyhedral, amorphous (A166137, A166138)

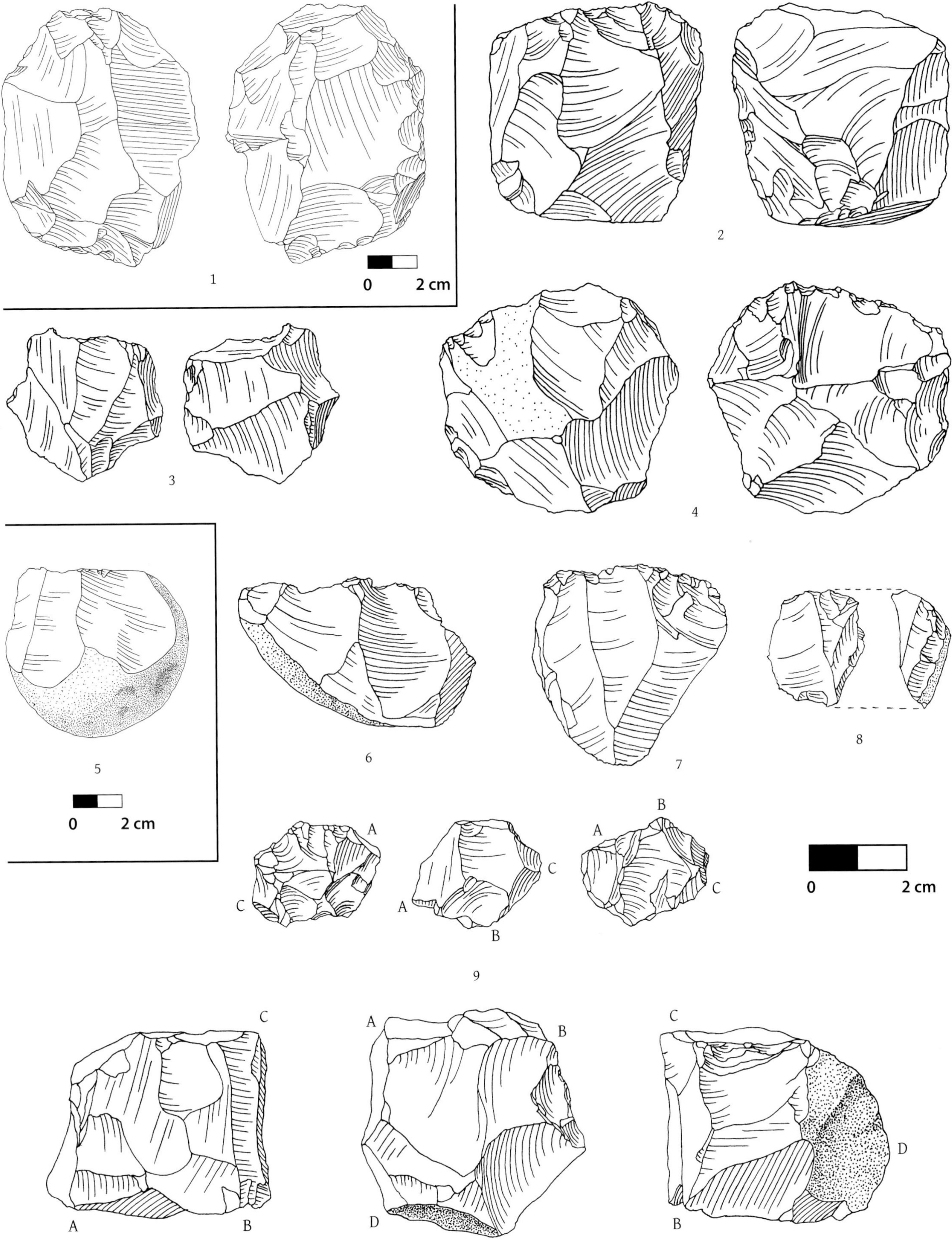
1
0 2 cm
2
3
4
5
0 2 cm
6
7
8
A
C
A
B
C
B
A
C
0 2 cm
9
C
A
B
A
B
D
C
D
B
10

Plate 15a

A

B

Artifacts associated with the monolith, photos and drawings. A: Artifacts in situ in part of monolith exposed below ground level: (*1–2*) pebble core fragments (A166139, A166140); (*3*) polyhedral core (A166141); (*4*) notched flake (A166142). B: Artifacts in situ in decomposing conglomerate around base of monolith: (*5*) hollow scraper (A66553); (*6–7*) notched flakes (A166143, A166144)

A

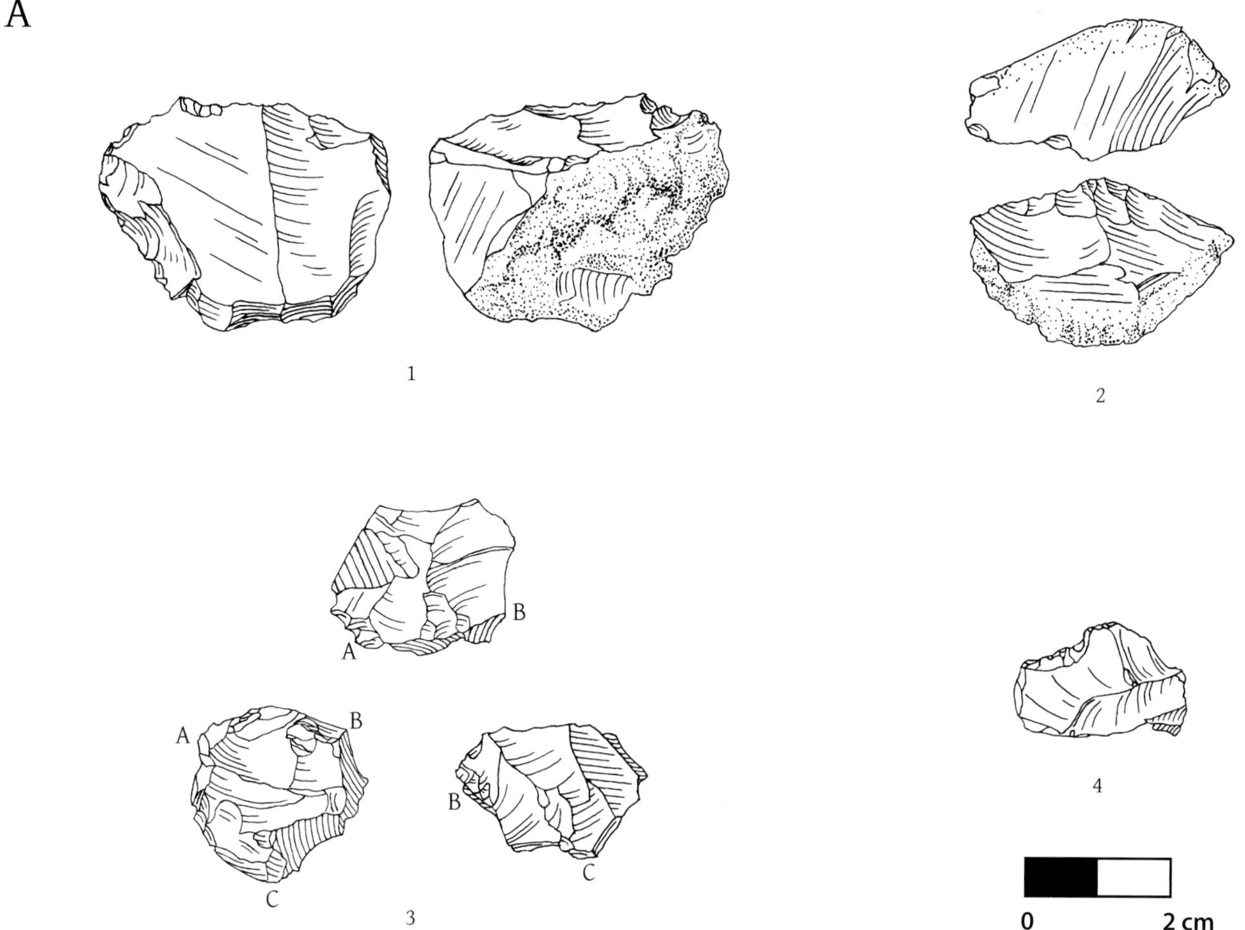

B

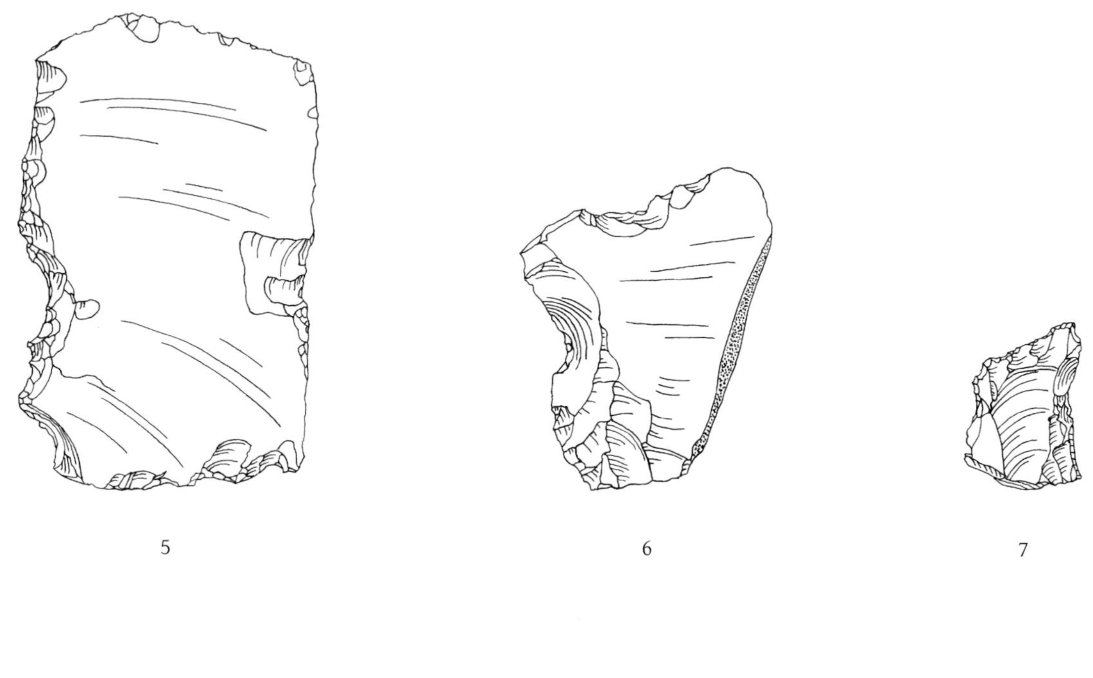

Plate 16

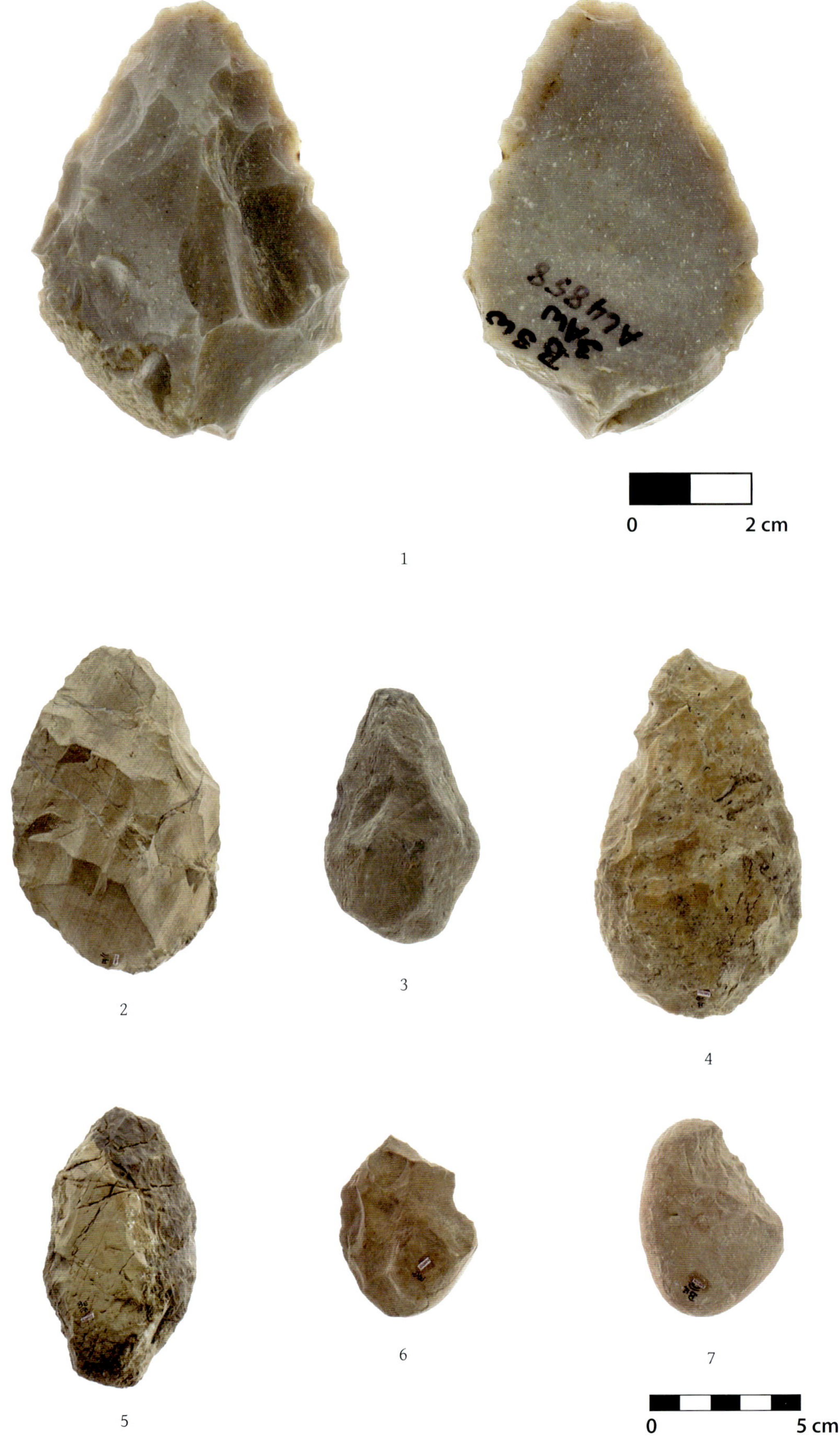

(*1*) Biface with traces of human blood (A64858). Further examples of (*2–6*) bifaces (A66500, A66501, A66502, A66503, A66505) and (*7*) a pebble chopper (A66506)

Plates 17–22. Reference photographs of the Barda Balka objects stored in the Oriental Institute Museum Archives, intended to provide the reader with an idea of the scope of the Barda Balka collection held by the Institute

Reference photographs of the Barda Balka objects stored in the Oriental Institute Museum Archives

Reference photographs of the Barda Balka objects stored in the Oriental Institute Museum Archives

Plate 20

Reference photographs of the Barda Balka objects stored in the Oriental Institute Museum Archives

Reference photographs of the Barda Balka objects stored in the Oriental Institute Museum Archives

Reference photographs of the Barda Balka objects stored in the Oriental Institute Museum Archives